ROUND THE NEXT CORNER

Other Publications
Advice To A Player
Acting My Way
Making The Stage Your Career

Anthology
Choosing Your Piece

Memoirs
Eleanor: Portrait of a Farjeon
Finding My Way

Poems
The Chastening

ROUND THE NEXT CORNER

A LIFE STORY

by

DENYS BLAKELOCK

with a Foreword

by

PAUL SCOFIELD

LONDON
VICTOR GOLLANCZ LTD
1967

Printed in Great Britain by
The Camelot Press Ltd., *London and Southampton*

For
Larry
by way of explanation

LIST OF ILLUSTRATIONS

ACKNOWLEDGMENTS

The Author wishes to acknowledge his indebtedness for the use of letters and the reproduction of material to the following: Mr. Noël Coward, Mrs. Herbert Farjeon, Mr. Albert Finney, Mrs. Christopher Hassall, Sir John Gielgud, Miss Nora Nicholson, Sir Laurence Olivier, Mr. Paul Scofield, Sir Donald Wolfit, and to the publishing houses of Victor Gollancz Ltd., William Heinemann Ltd. and W. & G. Foyle Ltd. Special mention should be made of Mr. Kerrison Preston, who has kindly allowed him to quote freely from *Letters from Graham Robertson*, published by Hamish Hamilton Ltd.

FOREWORD
by
Paul Scofield

IT WOULD SEEM to be an easy task to write a Foreword to a book written by a man one admires. But when his qualities and gifts are as subtle and as self-effacing as those of Denys Blakelock it is not easy at all.

In his book, *Finding My Way*, Mr. Blakelock wrote a luminous account of spiritual revelation in his own life. With simplicity he made a statement of faith; and it is with equal simplicity that he tells of his life in the theatre.

The Author has for many years been well known to theatre audiences as an actor with an immaculate style of high comedy; and for a certain shrewd humanity and the evidence in his acting of both intellect and feeling.

More recently his energies have been devoted to the guidance of young talent; and many of his pupils, established and with mature careers, continue to avail themselves of his professional wisdom and to enjoy his personal wit.

His story reflects his own balance between contemplation and involvement: a precarious poise, which, both passionate and tolerant, can be recognised as the authentic stance of the theatre.

AUTHOR'S PROLOGUE

OVER THE LAST ten years I have written six books. Each of them has been short and was written with a purpose of its own and a special kind of reader in mind. Each one could be described as autobiographical, in that I went for my material to my own personal experiences.

This book is a full-length life story and is intended for a wider and more general circle of readers. It is not just an actor's reminiscences, although I was an actor and nothing else for many years. But, being never in my heart entirely committed to that life, I gave it up for good at a critical peak in my progress, just at the point when I believe I had discovered that incommunicable secret of relaxation in the art of acting which is every player's aim.

Part II of this book is an account of the things that happened to me after I left the stage in 1954. It tells of the secondary vocations and the many surprises I found waiting for me round the corners.

This book forms a kind of trilogy with *Finding My Way* and *Eleanor: Portrait of a Farjeon*. It is not a sequel, since it runs concurrently with the other two. It borrows freely from its predecessors and also from the acting books, as the material used in them belongs to the same stretch of years.

I would have preferred to confine the book to the purely professional side of my life, dismissing anything serious or personal in a few sentences here and there. But when I did just this it was pointed out to me that the backbone of the story was missing; that the reader should not be left in the dark as to why my life took such a strange and unexpected course, why the behaviour-pattern has seemed to many so eccentric and unpredictable.

I have, therefore, begun at a point earlier than I intended and have written, as objectively as possible, something about the events and influences that proved to be the root cause of all that happened later.

D. B.

PART I

CHAPTER I

QUEEN VICTORIA AND I missed each other by six months. She died in the January; I was born in the June.

I was brought to birth against the background of the Boer War, escaped by one year fighting in the 1914 War and was rejected as unfit for World War No. 2. My life has been lived to the accompaniment of wars: wars without and wars within.

I was born into a clergyman's family and we lived in North London. There was a little money coming from my mother's side, so that we had nurses, governesses and "servants" to wait on us and spoil us. The servants were paid a sweated-labour wage; slept three together in a small room at the top of the house; got up at six o'clock and were on call until they went to bed at 10.30. They had one half-day off a week and half of every other Sunday. I think with affection and gratitude of those servants; many of them were the best friends I had in my young years.   I would like, if I could, to apologise to them for the life of un-complaining semi-slavery they lived in our service.

My father and mother were kind people. They intended nothing but good towards those who worked for them. It simply did not occur to the employers of domestic servants in those days that the conditions were bad. It was just in the recognised order of things.

I myself was a typical product of that kind of clergyman's family in the Victorian-Edwardian era. Although I had missed the Queen's reign, I did not escape its influences. My parents had been its victims and I in turn was theirs.

They had been curiously inconsistent, those Victorians. With women's evening frocks, for instance, it was *de rigueur* that they should be off the shoulder, and the breasts all but exposed. On the other hand ankles must be concealed by crinoline or pantalettes and the buttocks' shape hidden beneath a wadge of petticoats, and, later, by the bustle.

> "That which was chaste above the waist
> Was improper below the knee"

was a good summing up.

Pregnancy—so airily used nowadays—was a word that was **never** uttered; and, one might add, a condition that was never spoken of; but "coming event" was coyly whispered in the privacy of the powder room. The "loo" and the "toilet" were expressions unknown. In fact ladies and gentlemen just did not visit such places.

Sex was sacred—but profane. The body was the temple of the Holy Ghost and a thing of beauty, provided it appeared sexless, as in the Pre-Raphaelite paintings. But any reference to its component parts or any knowledge of their functions was taboo.

This attitude of false modesty covered up the devil only knew what of prurience and pretence and was inevitably handed on as a bad debt to the young Edwardian. I grew up more like a mouse than a man; but a mouse with the appetites of a tiger. On another plane, perhaps, I more resembled a sparrow; one that longed to open his tail like the peacock and display his plumage and be admired. This was because very early on my normal ego was suppressed by a combination of circumstances in our family life. Any sign of healthy male aggression met with opposition at home and was bullied out of me at school. I became timorous and diffident, supersensitive to unpopularity and acutely conscious of the world as a hostile place.

My upbringing was a strictly religious one and of the old-fashioned, Protestant variety. My father was a Church of England clergyman, himself the son of a Victorian country parson: the Rev. Clement Ogle Blakelock, rector of Shelfanger, a village outside the market town of Diss in Norfolk. This paternal grandfather of mine, tall, handsome, stern and sentimental, ruled his family after the pattern of the Rev. Patrick Brontë and Edward Moulton Barrett, with a mixture of love and fear which can sow such seeds of anxiety in the minds of children. They were sown in the mind of my father, who, to the day of his death at seventy, was afraid of the dark and always had a nightlight burning in his bedroom. He had an over-scrupulous, worrying mind, burdened amongst other things with the idea that sex was sacred and somehow sinful at the same time. You could never fail to make him laugh with a lavatorial, schoolboy joke; but the moment you moved into the terrain of the *double entendre* and the sexually symbolic his face became at once grave and you knew you had gone too far.

The seeds of anxiety planted in my father's mind became seeds of disaster in mine. This ambivalent conception of sex, especially, inevitably handed down to me, was to wind around my life a skein of entanglements so complex that it took the best part of forty years to unravel.

One element in the upbringing of those days, with which I found it particularly difficult to come to terms, was the mixture of parental benevolence and parental severity as shown by my father and mother. Their unpredictable displeasures and the disciplines thought proper in a Victorian parent were a constant source of confusion and bewilderment. They left me with a feeling of insecurity and a deep-seated distrust of the constancy of human affections. As I grew up, however faithful the friend or lover, I saw a threat to happiness in the slightest diminution of demonstrativeness and in every subtle change of expression on the face of love. It was inevitable, in my human relationships, that I should be possessive and demanding in love, and in friendship find it difficult to share my friends with other people.

One day, before I went away to school, I had an extraordinary conversation with my father. He sat at the desk in his study looking embarrassed and distressed. He was doing his best to warn me of the perils that beset a young boy on entering a public school.

There was much talk of "bigger boys", but it was so vague that it only served to make me exceedingly curious. It left me in regard to sex singularly ill-equipped for the world at large later on; but at least as far as school was concerned it put me on my guard against *something*.

There was no lack of romantic friendships in my schooldays. But I was particularly fortunate in the older boys I met. One, I remember, sent me a volume of Tennyson's poems and wrote of the love that surpasseth the love of women. If the love of man for man led to nothing more complicated than this no harm could be done. Anyway, I passed through my days at school unscathed—just another *Eric or Little by Little*. I remained so into my late twenties. Such innocence—or ignorance—proved, I fear, to be a doubtful blessing and in these present days would be hardly possible; or permitted by those who have to do with the bringing up of children.

If my father was vague and hesitant about the sex-instruction of his sons, my mother was completely silent on the subject. In fact, when questioned about it by someone more realistic, concerned for our welfare, she replied, "My boys never think about such things."

However, I look back, not in anger, but with nothing but affection and gratitude towards my parents: affection because they were both endearing characters in their very different ways; gratitude because in these perplexing days I appreciate more than ever the solid Christian beliefs they gave me, which I still hold and without which I should never have found even the degree of interior peace that is with me now.

CHAPTER II

WHILE MY FATHER'S family life was going on in Norfolk, across the country in Cambridge a rich, eccentric old lady was turning night into day; sitting down to dinner at midnight; playing chess into the small hours and writing angry letters to her servants. This was my maternal grandmother who, after my grandfather's death, had married again—a Mr. Amos, himself a widower. He in his turn died and his death provided the occasion for an angry letter. This time it was to the gardener, whom, on the morning after Mr. Amos had breathed his last, she saw from her bedroom window rolling the gravel path. Half an hour later the unfortunate man received a letter asking him: had he no heart, that he could erase those beloved footprints from the path before his late master was even in his grave? This would have been previous to the reading of Mr. Amos's will, which revealed his wish to be buried, not in Cambridge, but up in London side by side with his first wife.

My grandmother, not unnaturally, was piqued at this, and although she attended the local service she refused to follow Mr. Amos to London and be present at the final committal. Instead, she went to the cemetery at Cambridge and placed some flowers on the grave of her previous husband, Mr. Pike. Having fulfilled this labour of love, she was about to return to her carriage when she espied across the cemetery a "pauper's funeral". She immediately decided to join it, feeling no doubt that any service was better than no service at all.

So while Mr. Amos was being interred elsewhere, his widow, in her "rich weeds" (the Cranfordian description of an aunt who told me the story), stood looking down into the unknown pauper's grave, surrounded by the unknown pauper's poor relations.

The house in Cambridge where this grandmother of mine lived was called Paston House. It had been built out of the proceeds of the sale of the famous Paston Letters to the British Museum. This house played a very important part indeed in those early days of mine; and it seems to me now that I spent the greater part of my childhood in it, since the memories and impressions of all that took place there are far more vivid and more numerous than the things that happened in my own home.

Certainly my grandmother's was the sort of household to provide the maximum of excitement to a small child brought up rather frugally in a London suburb. Paston House stood in Bateman Street, with the Botanical Gardens on one side and my grandmother's stables on the other. She kept a handsome carriage-and-pair; also a little pony-carriage; and a yellow and black trap known as the Tub, drawn by the cob, a frisky young horse with an unfortunate habit of bolting, which on one occasion was nearly the end of me.

In *Eleanor* I gave a description of the inside of the house and of some of my memories and impressions of it.

"Aladdin's cave could not have been more intriguing to him than the inside of Paston House was to me, with its dark, shadowy hall and tall, winding staircase; its long, mysterious corridors, innumerable rooms and unexpected corners to be explored. I remember best the large drawing-room on the ground floor, with its many french windows opening on to the lawn; and, at night-time, the huge, glittering chandelier which made everything downstairs seem cheerful and friendly.

But by day or by night, up there at the top of the stairs, at the end of the passage, there was something I did not like. My grandmother was there . . . and she was not alone. She was ill, helpless . . . and in the power of Someone . . . Someone I hated . . . and who hated me . . . tall, dark, forbidding; and I was frightened . . . frightened, but fascinated too.

The plain facts were that by this time my grandmother had become a confirmed invalid; and though not actually bedridden spent most of her life in her own room. Her brief and infrequent appearances were made in a wheel-chair, in which she was taken down by an old-fashioned lift worked with ropes into the library, and so to the drawing-room or out into the garden. In these circumstances she had to have a trained nurse always in attendance. This nurse *was* tall, dark and rather severe-looking; and no doubt, placed as she was, she had a great deal of influence with my grandmother and very considerable power over the household. Moreover, I recollect quite clearly being given to understand that she did not like children; and I have an impression of occasions when I would come up against her, incur her displeasure, or suddenly find that menacing figure frustrating me as she towered above me on the stairs.

There was one particular period at Paston House which left an indelible imprint on my mind: a period of most unhappy associations for me. I had some serious illness and was left behind, this nurse of my grandmother in charge, while my parents and all the family returned to London.

Suddenly everything was changed. Gone were the familiar faces, the friendly voices, the excitement and the bustle I had known. Everyone had gone . . . I was left behind. There I was, up at the top of that vast house, alone and helpless in a darkened room, in the power of that inimical personality. No Babylonian captive could have felt more desolate than I did then. The waters of separation flowed over me, a blanket of impenetrable melancholy came down upon me, and I could do nothing.

Although in the cold light of adult reasoning it is easy now to dispel the shadows of that fantasy-world, nevertheless one must admit that there was plenty of material there for a child's mind to build upon. And I have very little doubt that it was in that house and at that period that I acquired my exaggerated fear of darkness, of being shut in; of being cut off from those I love and from safe, familiar ground; of being immobilised and helpless; of being in any way under compulsion or duress."

All these interrelated fears were to have an important bearing on the things that happened to me later. The seeds of claustrophobia had already been planted earlier. I had been given to sleep-walking; and in order to put a stop to this dangerous habit they had put me to sleep under a net from which there was no escaping, however acute the anxiety that was driving me. This device no doubt brought the somnambulance to an end but at what cost it is not hard to imagine. The cost was paid by me, as various symptoms revealed themselves in a hundred different ways as the years went by.

It was when the day came for me to be sent to one of the smaller public schools that they first began to make themselves plain. How dreadful going away to school for the first time was to me! The desolation of the ending of a love relationship, with its constant reminders of the little daily things that were shared and now must be done alone, is bad enough. But the intolerable anguish of homesickness in the very young runs it a good second.

My father took me down on that first day. I shall never forget saying goodbye to him half-way between the station and the school; nor the returning to my House, the long term stretching out like a desert before me, to see the iron railings and the heavy gate, which would be locked at night, barring the way downstairs from the dormitories.

Separation . . . enclosure . . . inimical people around me. Already the old situation was repeating itself. However, we are self-defensive animals; somehow I rose above it and settled down to the business of being turned into an English Public Schoolboy. But I was just not the type and never would be. I came up against the masters; I fell foul of most of the boys. The masters disapproved of me, because I was lazy, dreamy, and only worked under the threat of the "potty-bat"; the boys disliked me because I refused to lie low, as the Matron had advised me, because I flouted their conventions and generally behaved in a manner not seemly in a new boy.

There is one experience in my schooldays which must be mentioned, for it is an important signpost. The episode to which I am referring happened as a result of my unpopularity when I was a new boy. On the last Sunday of the term, when Satan always found work for sadistic hands to do, the boys in my House forced me, doubled almost in two, into a locker about three feet tall by two feet wide. This would have been disagreeable enough to a boy of normal reactions; but to me, with the claustrophobic symptoms already strongly developed, it was horror unspeakable. But speak I did. I imagine the horrific cries that were emitted from the dark interior of that locker would have frozen the blood-stream of the most hardened Grand Guignol audience. It was certainly too much for the little group of Public School bullies; and I was instantly released.

It is not on the whole surprising that I was filled with a sickening sense of dread at the thought of having to return to school at the beginning of each fresh term; and on one of these occasions I drank some camphorated oil, because the bottle was marked *Poison!* Although I did not intend anything as serious as suicide, I did hope to make myself ill enough to prevent my being sent back to school. I remember looking out through the lead-paned window of my mother's bedroom at the blinding rain and the grey skies with no break in the clouds to be seen anywhere; and I remember saying, simply and without melodrama, that I would rather die than go back that night. I can hear my mother's reply as she said reproachfully, "Oh! Denys, how *could* you? Think of the Armenians!"

(The Armenians at that time, during the First World War, were suffering similar persecutions and atrocities to those with which we have become so painfully familiar in more recent years.)

Does it really help to think of others in a worse plight than oneself? Not much, I fancy, when things are bad enough. The thought of the weight of human suffering pressing down upon the world has always seemed to me to make one's own troubles more acute.

The first Sunday sermon I heard at school was preached by a bearded clergyman with a fog-horn delivery. In this booming voice he gave out the text: "Lord, it is good for us to be here." I did not agree. Words far more to my taste were those we sang on the last morning of the term:

Lord, dismiss us with thy blessing.

To add to my offences at school I was that most despised and rejected of objects, the boy who was no good at games. At that juncture in our social history, before and during the 1914 war, to the English "professional" classes gamesmanship was their god. Not only did you depend on being good at games for your popularity with boys and masters in the term time. But at home in the holidays you were harried to death by uncles and aunts and by your parents' friends, if you didn't carry home a clutter of silver cups and other trophies of the playing field.

What could be more natural, then, than that a "rabbit" like me should turn to a world where no one cared whether you had been the hope of your side in the First XI or had won your rowing-blue at Oxford? A world where, with your face, voice, manner and personality, you could win all the glory of which you had been deprived at school. It turned out to be not quite as easy or as simple as that; but in the very early days at least there was a good deal to satisfy the frustrated ego to be found in the life of a young actor.

CHAPTER III

ONE OF MY favourite fairy-tales when I was a child was the story of
the Princess who was shut up by her stern father in a tall tower where
her lover could not reach her. But the Princess had a beautiful head of
fair hair, so thick and long that she was able to plait it, and let it down
from the tower like a great golden rope. Her lover would stand below
and cry:

> "Rapunsel, Rapunsel, let down your hair . . ."

Then up he would climb, a Romeo turned cat-burglar, to find solace
in his beloved's arms.

When I was young a woman's "crowning glory" was her hair, and
every girl one knew wore it long as a matter of course. A strange boast
of many a woman of that generation was that her hair was so long that
she could "sit on it in her bath".

Golden-haired women always had a great fascination for me (I
think most *young* gentlemen prefer blondes) and in common with many
others I used to collect picture postcards of my favourite actresses, who
were nearly always fair-haired.

At a very early age I was taken to one of my first pantomimes. It was
Jack and the Beanstalk at Drury Lane. I wondered and wondered where
Jack went to when he climbed up that beanstalk. That was the thought
that occupied me most and the only thing I can remember about the
afternoon. And there was one other favourite fairy-tale which was
read to me and which I also saw acted as a play: *Rumpelstiltzkin*, the
story of the little dwarf that got the Princess in his power by spinning
the flax for her that she could not spin herself. Flax, golden and silky—
like the shining hair of my own Princesses of the postcard world.
Where did *he* come from, Rumpelstiltzkin? And where did he go,
when the story ended "happily ever after"?

Whether it was the sinister figure of the dwarf, disappearing into
some dark and dreadful region of his own; or the Prince, shinning up
the blonde braids of his Princess in the Tower; or Jack climbing the
beanstalk and stepping off it into a land of mystery and magic, to my
child's imagination this Never Never Land, where dreams came true
and fair Princesses were for ever rescued, had an irresistible appeal. It

was inevitable that, as I grew older and came to the playgoing age, a continued preoccupation with the mysterious and the romantic should find expression in a passion for the theatre.

Just as at children's parties I never wanted to see how the conjuror did his tricks, so at the pantomime, to know that the transformation scene was in reality brought about by an elaborately-planned lighting plot and a series of gauzes and trap-doors would have spoiled everything.

The theatre of today has surely lost something in dispelling this sense of mystery; in revealing all its backstage secrets and the private affairs of its practitioners. It would be impossible for the present generation of theatre fans to imagine the awe and reverence in which the stars of forty years ago were held. We stood at stage-doors, as they do, but we approached our favourites with the greatest veneration; and if we happened to see Phyllis Dare in Bond Street or Sir Gerald du Maurier crossing Berkeley Square, we seldom did more than perhaps follow them at a respectful distance, as I once followed Lilian Braithwaite down the Haymarket and up Suffolk Street, till she vanished into that Never Never Land that was just beyond the stage-door.

So there I was, in the Ever Ever Present Land of reality, living the life of a conventional English schoolboy, but with one eye always on that door into the Never Never Land of fantasy, one ear strained to catch the mysterious music and the murmuring voices on the other side.

The home where I was brought up was a Philistine one. My mother's attitude towards the theatre is plainly shown by a remark she made that was frequently repeated in our family: "What I like is a nice *piece* with pretty dresses."

One day my mother and I went to see Gladys Cooper in a "nice piece" in which she played her usual rôle of beauty in distress, and as the curtain (and her long golden hair) came down at the end of one of the big scenes, I turned, shaken, to find my mother as usual with calm, impassive face. I said, "Do you mean to say you're not the least moved by that?" "Certainly not," she replied, "and if I were, I should look about me and remind myself that I was in a theatre." She did not want a conjuror. She did not want to be spellbound or to be carried away by a magician into a land of make-believe and poetry. Her attitude was typical of many Victorians, who thought it tasteless and embarrassing to show emotion, and especially in public places. As Lord Chesterfield had written in the 1770's, "In my mind there is nothing so illiberal and so ill-bred as audible laughter."

So by Victorian standards also it was considered vulgar to laugh out loud. Even Lilian Braithwaite, who became a friend of mine later, however amused she might be, was never heard to laugh at a theatre. I went with her to countless plays and I always noticed this. In fact I once said that if Lilian came to see you in a play you could easily pick out her face in the audience, because it was round and white, always in a Box and never laughing.

Yet she had a great sense of humour and in her own home I often heard her laugh in her deep and pleasant way. But she was a Victorian, like my mother, and they would have both agreed with Lord Chesterfield that it was ill-bred to be heard laughing in a public place.

My dislike of knowing how things were done carried itself on into my life as an actor. I was never interested in the production side of the theatre, or in what went on between the stage manager, the electricians, and the stage staff generally. Even now when people say to me (as they nearly always do), "But I thought it was so badly *produced*", I never know what they mean, unless the faults have been very glaring. It is the acting I care about. As for lighting, as long as I can see the actors' faces I don't care how many baby spots or surprise-pinks have been used in the process. However, I hold no brief for this attitude and I read the words which I have just set down with shame. It was all very well for Sir Gerald du Maurier to know nothing about lighting and to say, "I'd like a row of nice, pink bulbs here, please", but by the time I came into the theatre different and better standards were coming into vogue and I ought to have concerned myself with them.

It will be seen later how deeply I was to regret this and how at sea I was going to find myself, when the opportunity to become a director dropped into my lap like a ripe apple and the apple had to be thrown away.

CHAPTER IV

AT THE TIME of which I am writing, just after the 1914 War, in the upper-middle classes to go on the stage was still considered a daring thing to do. The stage for a male was thought not to be a manly occupation; and actresses were looked upon as rather *outré*. This despite the fact that Irene and Violet Vanbrugh, Lilian Braithwaite and Sybil Thorndike, all daughters of the Vicarage or the Close, had by that time broken the ice. They were simply the exception that proved the rule. And how pleasant, my mother's friends would say, to be able to go and see women play who were such good actresses and at the same time such "perfect ladies" too.

"Actressy" was an adjective much in use in those days, when, it must be remembered, the blue rinse and the pillar-box red mouth had not been seen in our land. Make-up, if used at all, was employed with great discretion and under conditions of the utmost secrecy. With the result that a woman in whom the slightest suspicion of hair that was dyed or a cheek that was "rouged" could be detected, was quickly labelled "actressy". So different from our own times, when most women contrive to look like actresses and most actresses to look as if they weren't.

So the stage was a raffish world and certainly no profession for a gentleman. This attitude was soon to change, however. In a few years the Bright Young Things descended on post-war London. Moral standards began to slip, clothes to become more scanty and make-up to be used by women of all ages. An army of men (including *gentlemen*), disgorged from the forces, turned with relief to a profession which, after the tedium of war service, would provide them with a gay and fairly easy means of livelihood.

But the brief period that I have in mind was before the men had returned from the battlefields and the social turnover had begun. The war was only just over; for it was in the December of 1918, one month after the Armistice had been signed, that I turned my seventeen-year-old face towards what is now known as the Royal Academy of Dramatic Art, or the R.A.D.A. or RADA.

It was not Royal then and without its R, simply asked to be called Ada, which it frequently was by the frivolous. But generally it was known as Tree's Academy, or Tree's School, or just "the" Academy.

At that time my father had a curate, Ted Hincks, who had been an actor and for some years on the stage-management side at the St. James's, under Sir George Alexander's *régime*. He used to tell me fascinating stories of backstage life in that theatre. How Lady Alexander used to address him as "Hincks", as if he were the boiler man; but Mrs. Patrick Campbell would say, "Mr. Hincks, will you be a *darling* and hold this for me?" How Alexander and Mrs. Pat would discuss arrangements for the Theatrical Garden Party on the stage at matinées when they were bored, and somehow manage to play their scenes together at the same time.

Ted Hincks, before that war, had been at the Academy, and it was he who strongly advised me to begin by going there. By the standards then accepted it gave a fairly good grounding to the would-be actor; and provided, as it still does, an excellent *entrée* to the theatre world when the training was completed.

But first of all there was my parents' permission to be obtained and a promise of the necessary fees, then 12 guineas a term, now £110. As so often happens when one expects to meet with opposition to some plan, my parents' reaction was much less unfavourable than I had anticipated. My mother, to whom I spoke first, obviously saw me at once with my name in lights, appearing in one "nice piece" after another; and she wished me luck as I went into the study. My father's objections, which did not last long, were practical rather than moral. There was no mention of the Road to Ruin. He confined himself to pointing out that so far I had given them insufficient justification for thinking I could make a living as an actor.

My aunts, too, took the news calmly; but one horrified lady in the parish, in a desperate attempt to put me off my project, gave me a novel by Miss Edna Lyall to read. It was called *Wayfaring Men* and was the story of a man of "gentle" birth who left the path of respectability and became a touring actor. Undiscovered and unsuccessful, he was still travelling from one small town to another, ill, ageing and penniless, in the last chapter. But as I had not the slightest intention of ever acting outside the West End Miss Lyall's persuasive novel had no effect on me.

Nor did *A Peep Behind the Scenes* act as a deterrent: the tale of a well-born lady who ran off with a circus artist and lived to rue the day. I was not planning to be either a bareback rider or a lion tamer, and the well-born lady's tragedy left me with my resolve unshaken.

For the Entrance Test to the Academy you were sent then a selection of pieces from which you could make your choice. I went for Antonio's speech from *The Merchant of Venice*: "But little; I am armed and well prepared." You were also asked to do something that was entirely of your own choosing. To say that I blush now when I confess to what I chose would be an understatement. It was *If* by Rudyard Kipling.

With the enviable abandon and unselfconsciousness of the green and inexperienced, I looked the three examiners in the face and let them have it. But before I could get to the point of telling them how to treat those two Imposters, Triumph and Disaster, as Mr. Kipling thought they should be treated, a voice said, "Thank you, Mr. Blakelock—that will do." I was in.

The first path was chosen and I began the climb.

CHAPTER V

The Academy, when I went there in January, 1919, consisted of two Gower Street houses knocked into one, with the first floor drawing-room of each made into one big room, which was known as the Stage Room. It was used longways from front to back; one-third being taken up with the tiny stage and the rest with rows of chairs to seat the audiences of admiring friends and parents. Behind them was a Box where the Judges sat, whose hoarse whispers could be heard only too plainly by the wretched students struggling to impress them.

Mr. Barnes—later to be Sir Kenneth—was not there when I arrived. He was at the wars. Or rather, hostilities being two months over he was waiting to be demobilised. He returned at the beginning of my last term, in the Spring of 1920.

I always felt rather a humbug in after years when I found fault with students at the R.A.D.A. because they skipped classes or turned up with a speech not learned. I remembered only too well how I did exactly the same kind of thing myself. But perhaps it is just because I did, and so bitterly regretted it afterwards, out in the tough jungle of theatre life, that I felt all the more bound to play the disciplinarian.

My own tendency was to avoid everything that I found difficult, to shrink from any possibility of being made to look a fool. So I used to cut, for example, the fencing and the ballet classes. The latter were given by d'Egville, a name famous in the world of dance. How invaluable it would have been to have had behind me the ease and grace of movement which assiduous attention to just such subjects as ballet and fencing alone can give. These are now compulsory at drama schools, as also are mime and movement.

Whatever may or may not be the arguments for the much-discussed Method classes, there is no doubt that work of that kind, if only viewed as an exercise, must be of the utmost aid to those who, as I was, are in any way tied up or inhibited by self-consciousness.

However, I do remember attending instruction in something called the Delsarte method. I believe it sprang from the school of dancing and movement started by Isadora Duncan. But by the time it reached me it seemed to consist mostly in learning how to fall; and, having fallen, to present a graceful picture. Now, of course, one feels it would be of little use. A modern producer would want a falling actor to end upside down and looking as stark and unbeautiful as possible. And he would be right; we are supposed to be holding the mirror up to nature and nature in such matters is not pretty. In those days there seemed to be a general tendency to beautify, to sentimentalise everything in dramatic art.

The Delsarte method was taught us, I remember, by a strange, intense lady who was dressed always in skin-tight black velvet, and had copper-coloured hair which would have been thought more than a little "actressy" by my family friends, I fear. In addition to the art of falling I learned from this instructress one other lesson I have not forgotten: never, never to be seen for one second on the stage in a serious part *on all fours*. You may have to go down upon your knees in prayer or in passionate supplication, but the moment you bend forward and put your hands to the ground you become a comic figure.

Alongside those early days of training as a professional actor, I was for the first time tasting blood and getting the smell of the sawdust through the only amateur activities I ever took part in.

In the early winter after the Armistice I started to run a concert party of my own. We used to give entertainments for charities in hospitals and parish halls. I was not only the producer, but alternated between musical comedy juvenile and red-nosed comedian. I knew then for the first time what it was to hold an audience: to experience the feeling of release that comes to a diffident person, who suddenly finds he is able to project his personality and feel its power over other people, instead of keeping it locked up within himself, sterile and unused.

I mention the amateur phase because this natural instinct for comedy was to lie half-buried for a long time. It only fully revealed itself, in fact, thirty years later, when I played Mr. Posket, the title rôle, in Pinero's farce *The Magistrate* at the Arts Theatre in 1943, the part which finally established me in people's minds as a comedian.

There were only five men students, including myself, that first term at the Academy, so I had the pick of the parts. One I remember especially was the boy in *The Title* by Arnold Bennett. This play had been done quite recently at the Royalty and we were lent the scripts that had been used for the West End production.

Thinking back to that script, which even to handle had a thrill for me because it had actually been on the other side of a stage door, I am reminded of a not unimportant feature of theatre history. In those times actors were not given a full script to work from, but one that contained only the lines of the part they were playing. It did not

Paul Tanqueray

The Author at the present time

Dorothy Wilding

The Author aged 21

Mary Clare and the Author in *Spring Cleaning*, 1925

include even the speeches of the other characters with whom they had
to act their scenes. You had your own lines in full, but the barest
minimum of a cue from the other person. I suppose this was left to the
discretion of the typist, who generally gave you about half a sentence to
show when it was your "turn to come in". The script my brother was
given in his first professional engagement began with the cue:

"... up in a delicatessen store."

Not a very illuminating guide to pre-rehearsal study.

This custom, originating I suppose from mistaken motives of
economy, continued for some time to come. When I worked with
Oscar Asche at His Majesty's in 1924 he did give us at least the complete scenes in which we were concerned. But it was not until years
after that that West End managements began to distribute full carbon
or Roneo copies of the play to the whole cast. No doubt it makes it
more expensive, but the time saved at rehearsals is considerable. As to
the approach of the individual actor to his rôle and its relation to the
play, one cannot imagine the Moscow Arts Theatre, or indeed any
present-day producer in this country, imposing such conditions of
study on a cast as we had to put up with in the old days.

The Academy course, now a seven-term one, in those easy-going
times consisted of four terms. So I left the *Royal* Academy of Dramatic
Art, as it was soon to become, after the Public Performance in the
Spring of 1920. I made my first stage appearance on 4th May of that
year at the Prince of Wales's Theatre, in *Sacrifice*, an Indian drama by
Rabindranath Tagore—wearing a turban and the male equivalent of a
sari.

CHAPTER VI

WHEN WE TURN over the pages of a family album and see ourselves as we used to be, how often we have to laugh. So as I now flick back the leaves and see that fading image of the drama student walking down Gower Street for the last time, I cannot help smiling at the memory of what was then my mental attitude. Particularly towards this first part that I have mentioned and its possibilities, as they seemed in my young fancy; so sadly different from what they were in actual fact.

It was only for one performance—a special matinée. Yet, in my ignorance of the way things worked in the theatre world, I really believed that my opportunity had already come. If I could secure this splendid part I was certain that half the managers and agents in London would be knocking on my door.

I did get the part but needless to say there were no managers at my feet, no offers of any kind; though, considering my inexperience, I was not altogether unsuccessful. One good thing at least came out of it. Amongst a few favourable Press notices I had one that was derogatory. It was from the distinguished dramatic critic, William Archer. "Mr. Denys Blakelock would have been excellent as the acolyte, but for his defective enunciation."

I was hurt; I was puzzled; and it was quite a long time before I found a friend courageous enough to tell me that I had a "suburban" accent. I lived to be grateful to that friend and to William Archer. I began to work on my voice: first with Elsie Fogerty, founder of the Central School, and later with Kate Emil Behnke. They were the two most renowned teachers of Voice Production of their day.

At least this speech difficulty made me especially sympathetic with students when I came to teach Diction at the R.A.D.A. John Neville, in his Foreword to *Advice to a Player*, says that he "can vouch from experience for the truth of Mr. Blakelock's statement . . . that an accent can be got rid of very quickly—*with hard work*". The italics are his. They are mine too. I found my own bad vowel-sounds an unconscionable time a-dying because I had not worked hard enough at the Academy. Nor, apparently, could I have applied myself to the task when I went to Elsie Fogerty, since two years later I was sent by Lilian Braithwaite and Clemence Dane to Miss Behnke.

I did not have to wait too long for my first engagement. On 22nd July, 1920, I had a letter from Dennis Eadie asking me to go and see him that morning at the theatre. Eadie was in management at the Royalty, the little theatre in Dean Street which has now been demolished to make room for Big Business. They were doing a production of a play new to England called *The Romantic Young Lady*, translated from the Spanish by Helen and Harley Granville Barker.

It could hardly have been a more exciting beginning for a young actor of nineteen. Not only was Eadie's management one of the most important in London, but this piece marked the return to the Theatre for the first time for many years of Granville Barker, who was himself to produce it.

I can never be too thankful for the privilege, enjoyed by few actors of my age, of having watched this great director at work on a production. It was a bad day for the stage when Barker turned his back on all active participation in theatrical affairs, and retired to the study to theorise—however admirably—and to translate the works of others.

During a period when I was out of a job, I had a letter from Granville Barker in answer to a despairing one from me. He told me not to be downcast: to remember that *the things one learns outside the world of the stage are of the most value to the work one does inside the theatre*.

I have never forgotten those words; I came to realise later their great wisdom.

I lived through the next week or two in a dream of indescribable delight. I could hardly believe that I was actually rehearsing on that stage at the Royalty, where I had seen so many plays from those faraway seats in the last rows of the Upper Circle, which were bookable and cost only half-a-crown.

Granville Barker, as one would expect, was a perfectionist. Although I was not required to assume a Spanish accent, he pointed out to me that a Spaniard of the age I was meant to be would have done his military service and would be upstanding and smart, would click his heels and bow gracefully when he kissed his grandmother's hand. I remember, at home, marching by the hour round my father's empty church hall, in my endeavour to develop this deportment; and my joy when Barker told me, two or three weeks later, that he could see how hard I had been working. But he cursed me once because I rushed at something he was explaining to us all. Then he quickly added, for fear that my young enthusiasm should be discouraged, "Oh, I wouldn't have you otherwise".

On another occasion Granville Barker took me to task for making my entrance and crossing down to the chair arranged, as if I were in any room, in any house; instead of suggesting that it was a room in my own home, to which I was accustomed, having in it familiar furniture and objects that belonged to me. This was a subtle piece of direction of which the most up-to-date Method actor could not but approve.

However, not even Barker's production could make *The Romantic Young Lady* into a success. Too slight perhaps for an English audience, it ran for only about three months. As for myself, I was neither a success nor a failure, for the good reason that I never even appeared. I rehearsed in joyous spirits for nearly a month; and at the beginning of the week before we were to open, I developed disquieting symptoms of shivering and sickness. They sent me home early from rehearsal; I dragged myself upstairs to my room and fell into bed. The next morning when the doctor came my worst fears were realised: I had Scarlet Fever.

Not a very auspicious beginning to a career; but in fact a significant and prophetic one. I was to prove to be a self-destroyer. At every important moment in my acting life, when I had a specially good part or particularly wanted to be on my toes, I produced some symptom, large or small, which either spoiled my enjoyment of the occasion or prevented my fulfilling the engagement altogether. At the Academy, a violent attack of influenza had prevented me from competing for a scholarship which I was all set to win; this, my first part, was taken from me by an infectious illness; I invariably developed gastritis, laryngitis or tonsilitis in time for a first night; I had to give up my only star part in a film to have an operation instead; and I finally allowed my personal and private bogeys to push me right out of the theatre.

CHAPTER VII

Scarlet fever does not last for ever. The tragedy of my first engagement was forgotten in the excitement of the next one. Kenneth Barnes came to my rescue with an introduction; and one morning in the late autumn of that year I kept an appointment at the Garrick Theatre. It was with Louis Calvert, who was producing Shaw's *You Never Can Tell* for a season of matinées. A superlatively good actor of the old school, Calvert had just written a book called *Problems of the Actor*, which fortunately I had bought and read. I have always believed that it was that book which got me the part of Philip, one of the twins.

A B.B.C. producer told me once that the only thing that put her off an actor when he wrote in for a job was if he had failed to find out the proper spelling of her name, because it suggested a lack of intelligence on the writer's part. If our destinies can hang on so slight a thread, it is not hard to imagine that Louis Calvert, who by that time was a good age and no less vain than any other actor, was flattered that such a young man as I was able to talk intelligently about his recently-published work. There was another boy in the running, whose work the manager, Leon M. Lion, had seen; he had not seen mine. Nor for that matter had Louis Calvert. But it was my lucky day; Calvert settled for me.

Soon I was on the other side of the magic door again and the last memories of scarlet fever had faded away. I found myself rehearsing with Lady Tree as my stage mother and her daughter, Viola, as my elder sister. Bernard Shaw himself directed some of the rehearsals. I was at once struck by Shaw's charm and by his kindliness of speech and manner; so different from what one had expected from the personality that came through in his writings and his pronouncements in the Press.

One could learn a lot from Louis Calvert as a producer; and as an actor when the play got going. He took the important part of the waiter which he had created originally. When I had to rush at him and nearly knock him over, it was he who told me—with a certain amount of asperity—that some things had to be *acted* with technical discretion and not performed with the boisterous abandon of real life. And at an early rehearsal, one evening at Lady Tree's flat in the Adelphi, he taught me the value of stamping on a laugh in the middle of a line, in order to get a bigger laugh on the point that came at the end of it.

Lady Tree was a fascinating character, given to absentmindedness on the stage. She would keep referring to "My daughter, Viola", instead of "My daughter, *Gloria*", the name of the character Viola played. Even Lady Tree's dress seemed not quite with us. In fact, I was given to understand that it was not a dress at all, but a number of lengths of cream lace, pinned on in pieces each evening by her dresser.

Viola Tree was not, in my opinion, a good actress, until she learned much later to capitalise her own idiosyncrasies in the parts that Ivor Novello wrote for her. She could then be very amusing. But Gloria Clandon in *You Never Can Tell* was quite beyond her. I can remember the notice she had from Sydney Carrol in *The Sunday Times*: "Miss Tree in the first Act wore a hat which appeared to have antlers sticking out of it. It was an interesting hat."

When our short season of *You Never Can Tell* came to an end just before Christmas, my first "peep behind the scenes" had been a pleasant one and had by no means put me off the stage. On the contrary, I had learned a little about the technique of acting and something of theatrical procedure and custom, and I looked forward with longing for the next engagement. It came quite soon. Granville Barker reappeared upon the scene. He was to produce, for Grossmith and Laurillard at the Gaiety, *The Betrothal*, a sequel to Maeterlinck's children's play, *The Blue Bird*.

Is there such a thing as a "walking understudy" now? That is what I was in *The Betrothal*. It meant I had to understudy the big leading part of Tyltyl, played by Bobby (later Robert) Andrews and do nothing else. Nowadays, people seem not only to have to play small parts and understudy in one play, but understudy in several other theatres at the same time. This can cause havoc in the winter-time, when a 'flu epidemic is on the rage.

The most attractive feature of *The Betrothal* from my point of view was the fact that the leading girl's part of Mytyl was played by the most adored of all my golden-haired Princesses, Gladys Cooper. So now it was, "Good-evening, Miss Cooper", as we came face to face on the other side of the stage-door or along one of the dressing-room passages, instead of

"Dear Miss Cooper,
    Will you be so very kind as to sign the enclosed photograph . . .?"

Hair in 1921 was still unshorn, and in *The Betrothal* once again Gladys Cooper's tresses came tumbling down. I shall never forget the beauty of that particular scene, in the Palace of the Unborn Children, when the smallest of all found her mother. Up to this point in the action of the play, Gladys had been silent, and veiled from head to foot in thick white draperies. But now the moment had come. As the child's tiny hands tugged at the draperies and they began to drop away, she disclosed her mother-that-was-to-be, in a Madonna-blue dress and seated on a throne. As she took the child in her arms, this wealth of golden hair came falling down to cover her.

The little girl, for some unfathomable reason known only to the child mind, began refusing to kiss Gladys Cooper in the scene in question; and the only way they could persuade this small prima donna to go on the stage and do her bit properly was to keep the understudy standing by in the wings, ready to take her place.

Half-way through the run, there came the momentous occasion when Gladys Cooper, Ivor Novello and Bobbie Andrews went by air to Paris for a week-end. In those days flying was very different from what it is today and people were not accustomed to it. The whole party were ill on the journey over, which with other complications prevented them from getting back in time for the play. On the Monday afternoon about three o'clock I had a telegram saying, "You play for Andrews tonight." And for that evening performance and the next day's matinée, a charming young actress now well known as Nora Swinburne and I played the two leading parts in *The Betrothal.*

When it finished in the Spring of 1921 I had my first taste of waiting; of watching the post; of writing and writing again; in fact of the search for work. It was a long time too. But then I had grandly set my face against everything but London. It must be the West End or nothing for me. How ashamed it makes me feel when I think about it now.

And I had not yet been summoned to Windsor, to that Command Performance. Never mind. Royalty came to meet me half-way—in Gower Street. The then Prince of Wales was to open the new Royal Academy of Dramatic Art theatre in Malet Street, forerunner of the Vanbrugh Theatre of today; and I was invited to appear, with a cast of ex-R.A.D.A. students already established, in an excerpt from *Trelawney of The Wells.*

CHAPTER VIII

ADA HAD BECOME RADA and could now boast a fine new theatre of its own. On to its stage on the afternoon of that Royal performance poured all the important actors and actresses of those days. The first act of a new play—a play never to be finished—by Sir James Barrie, called *Shall We Join the Ladies?*, was the great feature of the occasion. It was a dinner-table scene, in the country house of a rich, eccentric old man. Round the table sat Sir Charles Hawtrey, Sir Johnston Forbes-Robertson, Irene Vanbrugh, Fay Compton, Marie Löhr, Cyril Maude, Dion Boucicault, who played the host, and many others; and round the table, filling up the glasses, walked Gerald du Maurier, as Dolphin, with exactly the right mixture of dignity and deference—the perfect butler.

I stood spellbound in the wings watching them. They were all in my autograph book at home, these great ones whom I had worshipped from the gallery or the pit. Now they were here, only a few feet away, acting on the same stage on which I myself had appeared half an hour before. The Prince of Wales had been there too. The lights had fused just after I had made my first entrance with Meggie Albanesi; and the Prince, with his informal friendliness, had come up on to the stage from his seat in the front row of the stalls to talk to us.

Meggie Albanesi, who played Rose Trelawney, was one of those rare figures that appear on the theatre scene from time to time. Although, like Stephen Haggard, her career was cut short by death at a very early age, her name has become a legend in theatre history as Stephen's has. There is a plaque in her memory just off the foyer of the St. Martin's Theatre. She could not have been at the Academy many years before I was; but already at the time of this matinée, in which we were the young lovers, she was an established leading player much in demand. I think I saw her act only once, in Clemence Dane's *A Bill of Divorcement*. The daughter of Carlo Albanesi the pianist, she was of Italian descent, and she had the olive skin and dark looks that belong to those of Latin blood. Her voice one remembers most. It had a husky, vibrant quality; and she was at her best in intensely emotional parts like Hilary in *A Bill of Divorcement*. I did not like her very much. She treated me as if I were the little boy from next door. But that is nothing to go by. I was only there because someone else had fallen out; and I was so overwhelmed by the important people I was playing with that my personal reactions to any one of them must be discounted. That gifted actor Ion Swinley played Tom Wrench; and an inimitable comedienne called Athene Seyler was the Avonia Bunn.

Dion Boucicault produced our excerpt and what a martinet he was, even though we were giving our services. He was very angry with me because I asked to be let off early to go and see an agent about a specific job. It was unfortunate, as I had already had an unhappy experience with him in my last term as a student. He had taken my class in a few rehearsals of *The Amazons* at the Garrick Theatre where he was playing. After about ten minutes of the first of these he stopped the proceedings and said in icy tones, "Will you go back to the Academy and tell Mr. Barnes that when you have learned Sir Arthur Pinero's words I will rehearse you." This was my first lesson in the importance of paying an author the compliment of learning his exact text, and not a paraphrase of its meaning. Playwrights spend many hours polishing and balancing their dialogue. It is not only an insult to them to deviate from their script in the smallest particular, but incidentally it makes it far more difficult for the actor concerned to learn and speak the lines.

Dion Boucicault was the husband of Irene Vanbrugh, brother-in-law to Kenneth Barnes. He was one of the great producers of those days and especially associated with the plays of Arthur Pinero. That author was himself a tremendous stickler for exactitude in the matter of words. No one would ever have dared in a play of his to alter an "oh" or omit an "er". However, Ronald Squire had an amusing story of an occasion when Pinero did permit an interpolation; but it was in the case of a revival and it was no doubt many years since the author had looked at his script. The play was *The Schoolmistress*, and Squire interpolated a line which evoked a roar of laughter from everyone present when he spoke it. Sir Arthur Pinero, who had not been there on that occasion, when he heard it for the first time stopped the rehearsal, came down to the orchestra pit and said, "Mr. Squire, who wrote that line?" to which Squire replied with supreme aplomb, "You did, Sir Arthur." The line was kept in. No one ever knew whether the author really believed he had written it or not.

The matinée of which I have been writing was on 27th May, 1921. In June I was sent to see John Drinkwater whose *Abraham Lincoln* was to be revived at the Lyceum. I met him outside in the street, and on the stairs leading down to the stage we ran into his father, A.E., who was to be our stage-manager. I remember being impressed at seeing Drinkwater, who was then a man of not less than forty, stoop down and kiss his father as he said "Good morning". We, in our family, had always kissed my father; but up to that time I had somehow felt rather self-conscious about it, as if people might think it peculiar and un-English. Drinkwater looked more like a kindly schoolmaster than a poet. But how often does a poet look like a poet?

I was engaged for the part, small but exceptionally rewarding, of Scott, the young soldier who has been condemned to be shot for being found asleep on guard. He had volunteered to do double-duty in place of a fellow soldier who was sick. Abraham Lincoln hears of this, sends for the boy and gives the order for his reprieve.

This scene was so beautifully written by John Drinkwater, so perfectly played by William J. Rea as Lincoln and its appeal so infallible, that whoever had the good fortune to play the young soldier could hardly fail to get a round of applause on his exit. But there came a period during that run at the Lyceum when I did fail to get it night after night. In those days exit rounds were taken for granted as something which added to the general success of the show. So much so that I was hauled over the coals for missing the round after this particular scene. I found out the reason for it: I was playing the part in a mood of self-pity. I was enjoying myself; in fact, being exhibitionistic. The moment I corrected this approach the exit round came back. So I had learned another important lesson: *that the moment an actor becomes sorry for himself he kills the audience's sympathy stone dead.*

Harcourt Williams was in that company and I remember him asking me if I liked my part. I said I did, but that I wished there were more of it. He replied, "Never do that. When you've got a good part, never wish it were bigger." I came to value the wisdom of those words. Quantity counts for very little in the theatre. Quality is everything. Many a long part can be very dull. Many a small one can be unforgettable. If people come round to the dressing-room after the performance full of compliments, but complaining that there was too little of you in the play, then that is something to be pleased about. So often I have worked my fingers to the bone playing a sizeable but boring or un-sympathetic character, to be rewarded at the end of the evening with, "You have got a horrid part, haven't you?" But I shall be writing more about that later on.

Now I want to return for a moment to the days before and during the 1914 war. Living in North London, we used to go a great deal to the Marlborough in the Holloway Road. This theatre, now a cinema, was at that time as much a recognised suburban "date" as Golders Green or Streatham.

I saw there every kind of entertainment, which included *Madame Butterfly*, by the Carl Rosa Opera Company, *The Two Orphans* (a famous melodrama), and Julia Neilson and Fred Terry, in *The Scarlet Pimpernel* and *Sweet Nell of Old Drury*. I remember the disappointment, having waited at the stage door after a matinée, of being told that "Mr. and Mrs. Terry would not be coming out between the shows". In the West End, in those days and right up to the Second World War, people did as a rule come out of the theatre after a matinée and go home or to a club, to rest and have some food. No theatre began before 8.30 and you had plenty of time to relax and even have a proper dinner. But in the suburbs, where the curtain went up earlier and you were far from home, many actors preferred to have a snack in the dressing-room.

The last piece I saw at the Marlborough was the most memorable of all because it was one that was to play a big part in my own career as an actor: *Mr. Wu*, in which Matheson Lang had made a success in the West End, with Lilian Braithwaite as Mrs. Gregory. When it came to Holloway the play must have been on its first tour. I do not remember anyone in it by name, except Lang himself, his wife, Hutin Britten, as Mrs. Gregory, and Nona Wyn as Nang Ping.

A family friend offered to take me to see it and there was a great deal of discussion as to whether I should be allowed to go. I was about eleven or twelve years old and did not know the facts of life.

The story of *Mr. Wu* is worth telling, if only as an example of the kind of play which at that time satisfied most people; and as an illustration of the fact that the standard of play-writing has improved out of all recognition since the days which I am describing.

The story is this: Basil Gregory, son of an English merchant in China, has been making secret love to Nang Ping, daughter of Mr. Wu, a powerful Chinese mandarin.

In the first Act, set in Mr. Wu's garden, Nang Ping breaks the news to her lover that she is going to have a child. She tells him that when her father finds out, in accordance with his Oriental philosophy death is her inevitable share of the retribution from which she begs young Gregory to fly. Even as he hesitates and she persuades, Nang Ping looks over her lover's shoulder and screams with terror. Basil spins round and, horror-struck, sees standing there on the bridge across the lotus-pond, the inscrutable, the implacable, the inescapable—*Mr. Wu*!

In Act Two Basil is missing from his home; Mrs. Gregory is distraught; the powerful Mandarin offers to use his influence in the search. And so it comes about that one evening the grateful mother goes, in trusting innocence, to Mr. Wu's palace, lured there by his promise to give her positive information of her son's whereabouts.

The rest of the play is taken up with the famous scene in which Mr. Wu plays cat-and-mouse with Mrs. Gregory, revealing by slow degrees his fiendish proposition.

Yes, her son is there, a prisoner in his house, bound and helpless in the torture chamber only a few yards away. He shall be released—yes. But at a price. The price is heavy. "An eye for an eye, a tooth for a tooth", says Mr. Wu. *The price is the Englishwoman's honour.*

Needless to say it all comes right in the end. Mrs. Gregory's faithful servant, Ah Wong, who must surely have represented China in the Olympic Games, somehow manages to throw a bottle of poison, wrapped in a scarf, through a high circular window the size of a dustbin lid. Mad with terror, Mrs. Gregory, conveniently left alone at that moment, pours the poison into her own tea cup. Death rather than dishonour. Mr. Wu, returning in order to observe that charming old Chinese custom of taking a "cuppa" with one's victim, sniffs the air and suspects the worst. But he makes a fatal mistake. He assumes his own death to be Mrs. Gregory's objective. He changes the cups, drinks and dies in agony. Happily, in falling, he strikes the huge gong, thereby giving the agreed signal for Basil's release. Mother and son stagger into each other's arms and totter together out into the night air of Hong Kong.

It was this last Act that made *Mr. Wu* a questionable play for me to be taken to. All the discussion that went on only served to whet my curiosity. I pored over the *Play Pictorial*, read and read again the lines quoted from that particular scene, and remained unenlightened. "What can a woman value more than her own life? . . . or the life of her son?" Mrs. Gregory may have been able to answer that, but I couldn't. What *was* Mr. Wu up to?

In the end I was allowed to go to the play, and it became in my memory one of the major thrills of those youthful theatre-going days.

About ten years later, in the Spring of 1922, Matheson Lang decided to revive *Mr. Wu* at the New Theatre. As a result of being bombarded with letters from me, Lang allowed me to read Basil Gregory to him and engaged me for the part. It should have been given to an experienced actor at a salary of at least forty pounds a week. Lang paid me for my inexperience six. But he was very kind and pleasant to work with. I always feel Matheson Lang could have been a great actor, but that he took things too easily when once he was established in management. He was too intent on making money and enjoyed the comfortable living that it brought. His voice was full and rich. With that and a good physical appearance properly preserved, his talents should have taken him to a theatre like Drury Lane, where he could have played Shakespeare and the other classics, and stood for something serious and lasting in the theatre. But it was not altogether Lang's fault. Shakespeare had not yet come into his own; he was considered death and disaster to the Box Office.

In *Mr. Wu* my attention was drawn to my toes. They were *acting*, I was told, by the stage-manager, who watched my scene with Matheson Lang every evening. I was wearing sandals, so this personal and private matter was disclosed. Should toes act? I don't know. What would "the Method" men say? From the stage-manager's description of the way mine were working I should think they were *over*-acting; and that in any case was a sign that I had not yet reached the point of complete relaxation, which should be the aim of every actor.

That autumn of 1922 I condescended at last to take my art into the provinces; but only because the piece, *Comin' Thro' The Rye*, was destined eventually for London. So I had my first experience of staying in sordid theatre "digs" in Claypit Lane, Leeds; and in Brighton, where in the fireless room on those chill mornings I sat warming my feet on the tea-pot.

The story, with its typical Victorian theme of hopeless love, misunderstandings and explanations that came too late, was an old favourite of mine. I had read the novel one summer term at school, lying in the long grass in the playing-fields, when I should have been immersed in *Round The World in Eighty Days*, or knocking up a cricket-ball at the nets.

Comin' Thro' The Rye, after it had done four weeks of comin' thro' the provinces, came to an end; and I had another spell of being out of a job for some months. But I had been spotted in *Mr. Wu* by a very important man: Frederick Harrison, the manager of the Theatre Royal, Haymarket. It was he who gave me my next engagement; and at that very theatre to whose stage-door I had followed Lilian Braithwaite not so many years before; the theatre that had meant so much to me as a young playgoer. There was always something special about the Haymarket. Apart from anything else it had one particular attraction for its poorer patrons: the Pit was bookable on the day of the performance. The Box Office was opened about eleven o'clock in the morning, and you could get your seats and go away and have luncheon in comfort before the matinée. They cost two and sixpence, and if you were in the front row you might have been in the stalls, which were about ten and six.

So the prospect of an engagement at the Haymarket was an attractive one for sentimental reasons as well as from a professional point of view. It was regarded as the Mecca of the actor of those days. It was grand, dignified, select. To be asked to act at the Haymarket was a sign that you were getting somewhere if you were young; and if you were older it was proof that you were an artist of some standing.

The play was unworthy of the Haymarket, although it was written by H. A. Vachell, author of the Harrovian school-story, *The Hill*, who was considered a good dramatist. Its title was *Plus Fours* and for improbability its story ran *Mr. Wu*'s fairly close. The leading players were just about as ill-assorted a pair as you could have picked: Aubrey Smith, the rugged, cricket-playing, clubman type (an excellent actor); and popular Peggy O'Neil, a roguish Irish-American comedienne with a Vaudeville technique. Sir Charles Hawtrey was to produce. A strange set-up indeed, it seems to me now. But then I was not critical—only grateful for a good part in a distinguished cast at such a theatre; and especially for the prospect of being directed by a man who was one of the subtlest and most exquisite light comedians the British theatre has ever produced.

I was disappointed. Hawtrey seemed dour and depressed and un-interested in the play. I learned nothing from him. I do not remember him once coming up on to the stage and showing me how to get what he wanted. I am sure he was not well; in fact he did not live long after that time. The only positive thing he said to me I have never forgotten. It crushed me so. The part I was playing required an American accent. Every actor knows that the danger to look out for with an accent is monotony. It is often easy to find one or two inflections that are representative of a certain dialect. But to keep ringing the changes on them alone makes for a fatal sameness of voice, and would be especially damaging in the kind of light-comedy scene at the beginning of a play with which I was concerned. With my inexperience at that time I was no doubt making heavy going of the American angle of my part. Sir Charles Hawtrey did not go into any details. He simply said in wither-ing tones, "Mr. Blakelock, Americans *have* got a sense of humour, you know."

But I remember at the first plotting rehearsal Hawtrey saying to Clare Greet, who played our landlady in the scene, "Think of some 'business' there, Clare. I know I can leave that to you." I was enor-mously impressed by his complete confidence in this old character actress, who was indeed brilliant and had worked for Granville Barker and all the good managements. From her I did learn something. Clare Greet had a wonderful biting diction. Her consonants were the sharpest and brightest I have ever heard. Nothing makes stage speech audible, vital and interesting so much as crisp consonants.

Plus Fours ran only about three months; but when I left the Haymarket, at the end of that my first engagement there, I was not saying good-bye. I was to return to that beautiful theatre many times. It was to be associated in my mind in fact, more than any other, with most of the important things that were to happen to me both in my private and my professional life.

CHAPTER IX

IN GOING OVER this story it is my sincere intention not to indulge myself in reminiscences of the luxuriating sort, nor to drop a single name without some purpose. The purpose being either to make constructive comparison of the present with the past as to theatre customs and procedure, to fill in a piece of history, or at least to acquaint the reader with some point of real interest that I am able to hand on from my own experience.

As to this theatre section, the last thing I want to do is to take the readers of the book on a tedious journey from one theatrical engagement to another, regaling them with an actor's anecdotes on the way. I intend to dwell only on those that marked a milestone or led to development of character; and to stop to consider those personalities alone who had something positive and permanent to contribute to the theatre scene and to the works of future writers on the drama.

But in case I should give the idea that these easy, early successes I have described continued uninterruptedly, I must say here that in between them I did my share of Sunday shows; of tryouts at the Q Theatre or the Arts; and of West End plays on which one pinned one's hopes only to find oneself out of work again after four or five performances.

This was all part of the beginning actor's life then, and an important part of his grounding. Later it was to widen out into other fields: films, radio, and television. In detail it does not make interesting reading. I mention it here only in a general way, that I may not give the impression that I sat at home waiting for the plums to fall.

At the point I have now reached, for instance, I had to change my absurdly grand attitude as regards the question of acting only in London. I went on tour—and a long one. Nineteen weeks of traversing the British Isles from top to toe, and ending up in Dublin and Belfast. Months and months of nothing coming into my current account compelled me to accept the offer of this protracted tour, and with no positive plan of a London production at the end of it either. However, it was very proper that I should do this sort of work for a spell; and I learned a great deal from having to act in a strange theatre every Monday night, and to audiences which were so completely different in their reactions each week.

The piece was a "costume" play about highwaymen called *The Honourable Mr. Tawnish* by a popular novelist, Jeffrey Farnol. The period was Eighteenth Century and I played a dandy, a fop—Sir George D'Arcy.

"Saw you him with your own eyes, Sir George?"
"Split me, Madam, plain as I see you."

will serve as an example of the dialogue and perhaps suggest the quality of the play. But on that tour I learned a great deal about period acting and speaking and movement; about the wearing of powdered wigs and costume; about the use of the snuff-box and the lace handkerchief; and the fighting of duels with the foils.

Dennis Neilson-Terry, son of Fred Terry and Julia Neilson, played the title rôle, partnered by his wife, Mary Glynne. Dennis was as handsome as his sister, Phyllis, was beautiful; but he did not possess an eighth of her natural talent for acting. I saw her splendid Juliet at His Majesty's with Sir Herbert Tree as Mercutio. Dennis as a young man was inclined to be stiff in the romantic rôles that inevitably came his way; but, like so many, as he grew older he developed into a good character actor.

His great-aunt, Ellen Terry, came to see him as Tawnish at Brighton. She sat in the stage box and we could hear her chattering all through the performance. I was not sorry when that tour finished in the June of 1924 and I was free again. I could never be happy for long away from my own home and from my beloved London.

It was only a short wait this time before I was rehearsing again for a play which appeared to have all the elements of a great success. Oscar Asche had returned from a long foreign tour to his old haunt, His Majesty's, where he had been in *Chu Chin Chow* for five years during the 1914 War. The play was *The Royal Visitor*, a translation of *Le Roi*, a successful farcical comedy that had been revived many times in Paris, with Eve Lavallière in the leading woman's rôle. It was played here by Yvonne Arnaud. The King, said to be based on Edward VII, was Malcolm Keen; George Grossmith Junior and Asche himself were in the cast; and an actor playing a small part who was to be a popular favourite in later years, Gordon Harker. I shared a dressing-room with a most amusing companion, also unknown at that time, but afterwards to develop into the Irish Shakespearean actor, Anew McMaster.

The production cost £8,000. We rehearsed for six weeks and ran for one. Why it was such a failure I do not quite know. Perhaps it was just that over here we had not yet learned how to play or produce French farce in the way we seem to have done since, judging by the brilliant Alec Guinness *Hotel Paradiso* and—more recently—*A Flea In Her Ear* at the National Theatre. In the latter case it was an inspired move on the part of Sir Laurence Olivier to invite a French man of the theatre, Jacques Charon, to come over and direct it.

The failure of *The Royal Visitor* left me stranded at a bad time: in the autumn when all the new productions were cast. But my moment was coming; and it was to be a big moment—that first special opportunity that every actor needs to bring him right into the forefront.

Things were very slow until before Christmas, when Basil Dean, the most influential director of that era, asked me to go and see him about a new comedy by Frederick Lonsdale which he was doing at the St. Martin's Theatre. Early in the new year I was rehearsing with the most "fashionable" cast I had yet encountered, headed by Edna Best, Ronald Squire and Cathleen Nesbitt.

It is important in connection with this play to set the contemporary scene; to remind the reader of the social background against which it was written and produced. Only out of that particular background could *Spring Cleaning* have emerged; which accounts for the fact that with all its brilliance it has now become as dated as the cloche hat or the hobble skirt.

It was now January 1925. By this time the post-war era of the Bright Young Things was well under way. Comparison is inevitable between that generation to which I belonged and the New Young who followed upon World War No. 2. The Bright Young Things broke out with a kind of hectic optimism. The Beatniks became unruly from a desperate pessimism. However, I was not concerned with analysing social trends when, in 1925, I pushed my way through the crowds and managed to make myself heard above the clamour. And what a clamour it was! A post-war delirium was driving the new generation into a frenzied search for gaiety and excitement. There was a boom in the theatre such as was seen after the Second World War. Night clubs were at their zenith, cocktail crushes were the rage, "treasure hunts" were inaugurated weekly and bottle parties came nightly into their own. Good manners were going out of fashion, bad ones were considered *chic*. Superlatives were used about everything—and about nothing at all. If you had stood still and silent for five minutes at a party, from every direction your ear would have been assaulted by phrases such as "terribly terribly sweet", "too divine", "too marvellous", "I worship it"; and later, under the influence of Evelyn Waugh's *Vile Bodies*,

"How too, too shy-making" or "Darling, how *frightfully* sick-making!"

This little world (for it was only a little world, though it never realised how small it was), was made up of theatre folk, *débutantes* and Mayfair smartees; with a generous sprinkling of cadgers, gatecrashers, lounge lizards and hangers-on of both sexes. And it was this world that Frederick Lonsdale chose to pillory in the play that gave me my first opportunity.

Spring Cleaning was of the same vintage as Coward's *The Vortex* and they ran concurrently. It was sparkling. It was new. To say, however, as one critic did, that it was "the wittiest comedy since Sheridan" was an overstatement. But *Spring Cleaning* is not without its importance, as it could be said that with that play the theatre moved forward several paces towards the Theatre of the Outspoken. It was full of witty lines and it shocked.

Edna Best—then a great favourite—played a Lesbian. I—an unknown—played a queer young man: the first ever to be seen in a straight play.

These lines may serve as an example of the dialogue:

Bobby (D.B.): You ought to have been a boy, Fay.
Fay (Edna): So ought you.
Archie: Why is it women like these fellows?
Ernest: I don't know, old boy. I suppose it's because they can say things to women that men can't.

This was considered very, very daring.

One man in London had the prescience to realise what was in store for me. James Agate wrote of my performance:

"I do not know quite how Mr. Denys Blakelock is going to fortify his soul against the ravages of his flutterling. Perhaps he should now play a plumber by way of antidote. In the meantime he gets shouts of laughter."

As for myself, though I was twenty-four and had then been in the heart of the stage jungle for five years, I had but the vaguest idea of what it was that I was playing. I did know—and I didn't. I knew there were people "like that". But I had no real knowledge of the implications of homosexuality. At school, as I have said, I had been another *Eric or Little by Little*; and *Eric or Little by Little* I still remained.

One very positive thing I learned in connection with *Spring Cleaning*: how to dress. A very useful lesson for an actor in those days, when not only were so many plays, like this one, set in a Mayfair *milieu* of white tie and tails, double-breasted dinner-jackets and lounge suits, which had to be faultlessly cut and carelessly worn, but even when one was rehearsing the same sort of standard was expected.

Basil Dean could be said to have taught me how to dress. He questioned me early on in rehearsals as to what I had in my wardrobe that would be suitable for the ultra-smart young man I was playing. I replied that I thought I had the very thing. He asked me to bring it down to the theatre and to put it on for his inspection. I know now just how out of the picture that common-looking suit must have appeared. Basil Dean, who was not given to mincing his words, said, with great sensitiveness, no more than that he thought perhaps it was not quite right for the occasion. A few days later his manager sent for me and said, "Mr. Dean would like you to go to Savile Row for your clothes—to Anderson and Shepherd." They were the *crême de la crême* of tailors and to Anderson and Shepherd I went.

The cost was enormous but the cut was impeccable. I remained with them until the war came that changed all values. But I shall always be grateful to Basil Dean and also to the smart young actor who understudied me, Patrick Ludlow, who taught me the minor details of shirts and collars and ties and evening studs and cuff-links.

All this talk of appearance must sound strange to the young actor of today. Yet surely they must still apply, when the play is a revival of Oscar Wilde, Coward or John Galsworthy?

When the Lonsdale play finished, in the late summer of 1925, my troubles began in earnest. The *Spring Cleaning* young man had set the fashion for that sort of character to appear in every third play that was produced. For the next year or two I was besieged with invitations to play him. I refused them all.

CHAPTER X

Before I go on to the next milestone perhaps this would be a good point at which to discuss someone whom I met about that period—in 1926: someone who was to play a big part in my life and indeed in the lives of all those who work in the theatre, or who now throng the box office for tickets to see him act.

At this juncture I was moving about in London's Anglo-Catholic circles and had particular connections with All Saints', Margaret Street. This fashionable church was well known for its sermons and its music. The latter was provided by a choir school and the most popular preaching came from Father Geoffrey Heald, who was highly artistic and a great theatre lover. He directed and designed flawless productions of Shakespeare with the boys, which were financed by the then Duke of Newcastle and no expense was spared. To one of these, *The Taming of the Shrew*, I was invited.

When I arrived to take up my seat I was impressed, being a very young actor, by my fellow guests, many of whom were distinguished actors and actresses of that time, including, I remember, Sybil Thorndike, then many years away from her D.B.E. But as the play began all else was forgotten in the remarkable acting that we saw from these small boys, especially from the one that was playing Katharine.

Although forty years have passed since that afternoon, I can see Laurence Olivier as he looked then as clearly as I can remember his Othello of only a year ago. He was not good-looking as a boy; he had a rather dark, glowering look, which was admirably suited to the Shrew. As to his acting it is of course not possible to describe it; I can only say that the impression he made on that very professional audience was something quite exceptional. That this is no exaggeration will be shown by the fact that the whole production was invited to appear at Stratford-upon-Avon in the summer, directly, I am sure, on account of Laurence Olivier's performance.

I did not meet him that day at All Saints'. Four years went by before we met. It was at the first rehearsal of Henri Ghéon's *The Marvellous History of St. Bernard*, in which I played the Archangel Gabriel and was also first understudy to St. Bernard (Robert Harris). Larry was second understudy; and he played a very small part as well. On the programme, which I still possess, he appears thus:

Minstrel   Laurence Ollivier

He must have been annoyed by the two l's, as I remember his being annoyed with me on one early occasion, when I carelessly introduced him as Laurence "Oliver". I should have been just as angry had he called me "Blacklock". But Larry got my name right when he made himself known to me at the Kingsway Theatre that day. "I think you know Father Heald?" he said.

That was the beginning of a great friendship: one that has lasted fundamentally, I think, as early friendships do; even if they are allowed to fall into disrepair through the pressure of responsibilities and though the paths divide.

Larry once told Cyril Cusack that I had "ridden into the storm" and he had "ridden out of it". This referred to the question of religion which was the most important link we had in common when we first became friends. Our fathers were clergymen and we were both Anglo-Catholics and very much at one in spiritual matters. Laurence Olivier was a deeply religious boy. But after his marriage and his first visit to New York with Coward in *Private Lives* he told me on his return that he could no longer throw in his lot with any organised religion. This was a blow to me. It had been a great bond and I myself continued to be a believer and in fact some years later became a Roman Catholic.

But during the *St. Bernard* period that was all in the future. Larry and I began to see a great deal of each other. He was always welcome at my father's London vicarage and I went many times to stay at Addington in Buckinghamshire where his father was the rector. The church, set in a private park, was small, ancient and very beautiful. Often I have seen Laurence Olivier serving his father's week-day Mass with no one else present but his stepmother and myself.

Down at Dymchurch, too, I stayed with them at their cottage which stood with a few others right by the seashore. The one next to it was called "St. Joan" and belonged to Sybil Thorndike. The accommodation in the Oliviers' cottage was limited and I remember that Larry and I shared a minute bedroom.

He always seemed to me like an only child. But I think that was because before I knew him, Larry's brother, Dickie, had gone abroad to work and his sister, Sybil, had married. He was very devoted to his stepmother who went out of her way to make things pleasant for him.

His own mother, whom he dearly loved, had died when he was a boy at All Saints'. Geoffrey Heald had had to break the news to him. Only this summer of 1966 I in my turn had to write and tell Larry of Geoffrey's death. When he telephoned the following day he sounded just as he used to sound all those years ago. The timbre of his voice and the way he spoke had gone back to what they were when I heard him say, "I think you know Father Heald?"

I mention this because when one is considering a man who is not just an old friend but also a public personality, about whom future theatre historians will want to write, I feel everything is of importance. The question of Olivier's voice, for instance, is an interesting one, because there seemed to be a definite point at which it altered. I noticed it for the first time in an early Hollywood film. It seemed to me as if he wished to acquire a mid-Atlantic style of speech: something that was neither British nor American, but a compromise that would be acceptable on both sides of the ocean.

To what extent this was thought-out I have no idea. It could well be part of Olivier's astute approach to his work and career; or it could come from his chameleon-like tendency to take on the colour of his immediate surroundings. In his recent contribution to the television series, *Great Acting*, I was interested to notice certain slight deviations in his conversational speech which were not present when I heard it last. It was as if his association with the New Wave theatre world had in its turn played a part in bringing about yet another modification.

In his Foreword to *Finding My Way* Olivier wrote that I was the first human being in his life that he could really think of as "my friend". He went on: "Having lived through my earliest days with a peculiarly desperate wish to be liked unanswered, I embraced this unaccustomed happiness with an innocent young gratitude...."

Reading this so many years afterwards I was touched of course but also surprised; because at the time it had never occurred to me that Larry was anything else but happy and a boy who was liked by most people who knew him. He was demonstratively affectionate, enthusiastic and interested in everything. He had superabundant vitality, a gift which seems common to all highly creative actors with star quality: that animal magnetism to which they owe their force and their appeal. The American actress Clare Eames, to whom I introduced Larry and who coached him in a Bowery accent for *The Adding Machine*, said to me at the time, "Larry looks down at me with the eyes of a conqueror." He was just beginning to be conscious of the dynamic power that was in him.

But to return to the question of his problem of being liked or not liked: looking back I recollect that Olivier could be very blunt in his youthful days, blunt and undiplomatic; and everyone does not care for that. I myself could appreciate it more now than I did then. Once we were sitting in a restaurant called the Cabin in the Strand, I with my hands spread out on the table. Larry looked down at them and said, "Funny stumpy little hands, aren't they?" He has particularly fine ones himself and I always wanted to be the possessor of beautiful hands.

On another occasion I was driving him out into the country. We were going down the hill from the Heath to Golders Green. I remember the spot, because this conversation had a tremendous importance for me. We were discussing a new play by John van Druten and Larry said, "I suggested you for the leading part in it but John said, Denys is a very good actor but *he hasn't got star quality*." Those last words went straight to my heart like a stiletto. I think it was the first time I had heard the expression; I know it was my first awareness of that un-palatable truth about myself. Larry was a kind and sympathetic character. He had no malice in him. This was simply said out of a bluntness which belonged to his family. His father was much the same and my over-sensitiveness would often be ruffled by remarks from Mr. Olivier which had no intent to hurt behind them.

John van Druten was right about me; and it was good that I should know the truth through Larry. I never had star quality, although it was proved many years later that I could carry a play in a big leading part of a certain kind. But that is not quite the same thing.

Larry, too, could be sensitive about his appearance, especially when I first knew him, before he had learned how to dress himself. He was once very cross with his father, who in front of a family gathering drew attention to his rebel hair. And I was no less irritated with my mother, who after Larry's first visit remarked: "A nice young man— but very plain." Thus she dismissed the future Sir Laurence Olivier; and put him to sleep in the boxroom when he came to stay. But she was right. Larry was not good-looking at that time. He had teeth that were set too far apart and eyebrows that grew thickly and without shape across his nose. He had a thatch of unmanageable hair that came far forward in a kind of widow's peak, and his nose was a broad one. He wore very unbecoming suits, much too old-looking for a young man. He told me in later days that these were cast-offs of an uncle, altered to fit him. I wrote in *Advice to a Player* of the remarkable meta-morphosis that took place in Olivier after his seasons at the Birming-ham Repertory Theatre, where he must have been able for the first time to put some money by. He turned up in London looking a different man. It is the supreme example to the young actor of application and determination.

"He had somehow got his hair to part at last; he had the gaps between his teeth filled in; his eyebrows trimmed and straightened; and he was beautifully and gaily dressed. He had stopped short at his nose, though he has made up for this since by remodelling it with nose-clay into one shape after another in almost every part he has played in the last twenty-five years."

But before this, in the days when we first knew him, Larry used to look rather pale. Perhaps he did not get enough to eat. I know he was living in a bed-sitting room in Maida Vale and doing without breakfast—a practice which I persuaded him to discontinue.

Olivier's innate kindliness and capacity for taking trouble over his friends will be shown by this letter written on board ship en route for Australia. I had sent him *Finding My Way* (in its original version) and this is the letter he sent with his Foreword and the manuscript:

> Monday, March 9th, 1948
> At Sea—between Capetown
> and Fremantle—South
> Indian Ocean

As from:
Old Vic Theatre Co.,
c/o British Council,
489 Bourke Street,
Melbourne, C.I.,
Victoria,
Australia.

Dearest Denys,
Here it is. I do hope it's all right for you. I have had to be working like a dog during this trip and it's been a bit awkward getting the whole book read—which I think was essential and I've been all day getting this done; and much as I'd love to try and do the whole thing again and much better, I'm afraid time is too short for me. We are having a marvellous trip—on a lovely ship. We rehearse four days at a time and then a break, which makes it feel a bit more like a holiday for them all than a seven day week, with a siesta midday for sleeping if hot.

Dear boy, until I see you, more or less all that I feel about your book I have written in the Foreword. . . . You said not to talk about it, so I didn't have it typed to reassure you of this, and have written it as plain as I could! I shall airmail this letter, the Foreword and the book *registered* all together from Perth—I presume you have another copy of the book and in case it's lost I have a copy of the Foreword.

Wonderful luck with it . . . I have cut one paragraph of my effort, but left it so that you could read it as it's a kind of private apology!

> Devoted love
>
> God bless you—
>
> Larry

Laurence Olivier never at any time had need to apologise to me. The apology should be on my side.

His were great gifts; mine were small ones, made smaller by a deep-seated and destructive diffidence. Larry was "committed", single-minded about his work; I was fundamentally half-hearted, having lower ideals then about the theatre than I have now. He liked, in those days, the social life of the stage so necessary to a really successful career. I liked it not at all.

Nevertheless, Larry always did his best for many years to include me in his life as far as was reasonably possible. He frequently, for instance, pressed me to go and stay for week-ends in the country. This presented a major obstacle; as by that time I had found that I was not happy sleeping in strange houses, however kind my hosts might be, and I would only go and visit friends for the day. I liked doing that; it was no more than paying a call. I knew I would be off again and my own master in a few hours. But to stay in a household, to my contortionist mind, always seemed to constitute a kind of curtailment of personal liberty. You had to conform. Moreover, I was a bad sleeper; and if I had to resolve the problems of insomnia I preferred to do it in the security of my own home. There at least I knew the lie of the land and could get up and wander about without disturbing other people.

This extract from a letter of Larry's will demonstrate the difficulty and show how kind he was in trying to dissuade me from my pusillanimous ways.

11th April 1950

Dear old Denys,

. . . quite understand about the week-end, though I'm very sad I shan't have the privilege of taking you to the little R.C. church.

We shall long to see you.
Route enclosed dear boy
                    Ever love
                         Larry

Although he was acting at night and would have had a long drive after the theatre, he was even prepared to be up early to drive me to my obligations. Could any old friend do more?

CHAPTER XI

There are many reasons why I am going to choose *The Silver Cord* as a play to pause upon; so many that they can be left to reveal their importance as this chapter progresses. The play, to begin with, was very "advanced" for its times, not in its form but in its theme. The observations upon it of two dissimilar men will give an indication of this.

When I told Geoffrey Heald the story of the play I remember him saying, "In other words it's about a mother who's in love with her two sons." And Granville Barker, seeing *The Silver Cord* in performance, described it to the manager as being "about the Oedipus complex". The manager, a business man, had no idea of what he meant. Neither had I then. It was early days to come out with the fine Freudian phrases which every amateur psychologist now throws off with an air of nonchalance.

I have already quoted some dialogue from *Spring Cleaning* and said that it was thought to be daring. This is a line from memory out of *The Silver Cord*, spoken by the daughter-in-law in a last Act showdown with the mother:

"And what you really want is to suckle him at your breast."

That too was considered very daring indeed.

Most of the public were fascinated; many were outraged. Angry mothers wrote furiously to the management. Grateful wives of "mothers' boys" expressed their appreciation. The play was a success.

The Silver Cord brought to London a remarkable actress already mentioned, Clare Eames, wife of the play's author, Sidney Howard. This distinguished couple were associated with the work done by the New York Theatre Guild and were therefore representative of all that was theatrically up-to-date in the 'Twenties. They introduced into our theatre at least one innovation: the abolition of curtain calls at the end of Acts. Up to that time the company had always appeared to make their bow at the end of each Act. Earlier still, having made their exit to a round of applause after an effective scene, they would come back through the door to acknowledge it. Even in my time, great favourites like Marie Tempest, making their first entrance, would stop and come out of the character, inclining the head slightly to acknowledge their reception.

The Howards would have none of that. Early on in rehearsals I remember Sidney Howard carefully arranging with Lilian Braithwaite how she could fill in in a natural way the interruption by the applause which she would inevitably receive from the first night audience.

My friendship with Sidney and Clare Howard and everything to do with *The Silver Cord* production marked the small beginnings of a new attitude in myself towards theatre work: the dawning of an idea, not to be fully realised for a long time yet, that there was something more worth while about it than just the exploitation of one's own clamorous ego.

During one of my many talks with Clare Eames I had my first whiff of a school of acting then for us in its infancy, now well known. I remember Clare telling me with a mischievous twinkle of a company of actors in America called *The Hedgerow Players*. They believed in going into a play in great depth and taking a long time over it. If, for instance, two actors were playing grown-up brothers, they would go right back to the start of things and get down on the floor and play with bricks together, as if they were in their nursery days at home. Clare, serious-minded and intellectual actress though she was, had a good deal to say about this that was frivolous.

I know now that those *Hedgerow Players* must have been in the vanguard of the movement of which we have since heard so much. Coming to us from America, it originated in Russia from Constantin Stanislavsky of the Moscow Art Theatre and we know it as "The Method".

John Southworth, reviewing *Acting My Way* in The Tablet, wrote as follows on this subject:

". . . My own view is that Constantin Stanislavsky must be gyrating in his grave at nearly everything that is being done in his name by the Method Boys. Having been trained in his discipline, I find it difficult to see any point of contact between what he taught and the so-called Method, the name of which is itself a contradiction of his ideas. The great Russian director was concerned with laying down a method of *training actors*, not a method of acting, which is nonsense . . ."

Lilian Braithwaite played such an important part in the British theatre over so long a period that it would be unthinkable to write about *The Silver Cord* without mention of her performance of Mrs.

Phelps. This splendid rôle of the possessive mother provided a vehicle for the employment of both facets of Lilian Braithwaite's talent: the strong dramatic style which she had already perfected, and the individual comedy, capitalising her marked vocal characteristics, which since *The Vortex* she had begun to make peculiarly her own. With her uncanny gift for subtle inflections she lightened the shadows of the unpleasant character she was acting and lifted the whole play on to a comedic level.

It was during the run of this piece that my friendship with Lilian Braithwaite first began. No young actor finding himself in a play with her could fail to respond gratefully to her friendliness, her sympathetic encouragement and her constructive counsel. Her wise advice on matters theatrical or personal was never forced on one, but was always there for those who had the sense to ask for it.

Lilian had a wonderful capacity for friendship, a gift of continuing to take trouble about her friends that is rare in the theatre world, where people tend to be most thick with those with whom they are working at the moment. She was not an emotional woman. In many ways she reminded me of my own mother; in that she loved to receive attention and demonstrative affection but never really returned it. She offered you a rather cold, unyielding cheek, and the idea of Lilian putting her arms round you in a warm embrace was unthinkable. Her wit, for which she was noted, had a keen edge; she saw through the weaknesses and eccentricities of her fellow-beings with deadly clarity, and the things she said about them were frequently quoted. But as many stories could be told of kind acts done and practical help given to those less fortunate than herself whom she knew to be in low waters. Once, when I was ill, she offered of her own volition to lend me £200. This loan I accepted and paid back within the year. She also sent me, as a gift, £25 so that I might have another fortnight's recuperation.

As far as my own career was concerned, *The Silver Cord* stands out above all others of my early plays as a landmark, though not for the expected reasons. Despite the improvement in my attitude towards the theatre through my association with the Sidney Howards, it was from that engagement onwards that I trace the start of my falling out of love with acting itself. I developed then a claustrophobic dread of long runs, audience-hatred and an uncontrollable hysteria on the stage which was to spoil much of my work.

The reasons for this seem plainer now than they were at the time. The fact was that the play, which had promised so much and seemed such a movement forward for me professionally, proved to be several steps backward psychologically, and was a source of disappointment and disillusion.

Up to that time I had had beginner's luck in the emotional, sympathetic parts I had been given, which had brought me just the adulation and attention my frustrated ego craved. But Robert Phelps in *The Silver Cord* was the first of a long line of weak, spineless young men that came my way. After the opening night it began to be evident to me that there was a change. I became morbidly conscious of English audiences' dislike of such characters, and their inability to separate the part from the actor. When you played a rôle like Robert Phelps you were passed over by the critics and ridiculed by the public.

This was not at all what I had gone on the stage to find. I had not become an actor to be despised and rejected. Was the sparrow not to be allowed to play the peacock after all?

I was not to know then that I was, in fact, only exhibiting the same behaviour-pattern shown by leading players like Marie Tempest, who insisted on any line being cut from the script that put them in an unsympathetic light. This is an actor's disease. I had it badly and was too young to be able to recognise it and certainly in no position to be able to do anything about it if I had.

Paradoxically I, too, identified myself with the part. The problems and depressions of the melancholy Robert, condemned to live for ever in a minor key, rang far too many bells for me in the unexplored depths of my unconscious mind. This first path that I had chosen of an actor's life—and I could conceive then of no other—was proving a stony one. Under the soil the seeds of claustrophobia, planted in the early days, had put down firm and spreading roots. The weeds were thrusting upwards, destroying the healthy, smooth ground, obscuring the footway, making each step more difficult to take.

The sight most dreaded by actors is that of the notice of closure of the play being pinned up on the board. I, on the contrary, was always secretly glad to see it; and never more thankful than when, at the end of that long run, I read that *The Silver Cord* was coming to an end at last.

CHAPTER XII

PERHAPS THIS IS the point at which it is advisable to be more explicit: to say something more explanatory about the recurring theme of claustrophobia, which has been such an overwhelming influence in my life, and which therefore has to thread its way throughout this book.

Claustrophobia is something that is understood by most normal people to a certain extent; but only those who have had to deal with it as a chronic illness in someone close to them can know how far-reaching and destructive its effects can be.

The dictionary definition of the word is: *fear of being enclosed in a narrow or confined space.* This is inevitably an understatement. There is the claustrophobia of place as it suggests. But there is also the claustrophobia of the situation. The ramifications between the two are manifold. For myself *any* kind of curtailment of the most temporary freedom provokes symptoms of acute agitation.

As to place:
To be trapped in a lift between floors;
To be caught in the Tube between stations;
To sit in the middle of a row;
To stand in the centre of a crowd;

are some of the more obvious experiences the very possibilities of which I always avoid. I never go in a lift; and from the age of twenty onwards I ceased travelling on the Underground. My theatre seats must be on a gangway; and an early taste of being taken to the Lord Mayor's Show put paid to the occasions of great crowds for me.

As to situation:
To promise to play a part;
To sign a contract committing myself to an indefinite period;
To stay as a guest in a house for a specified time (as already shown);
To make a proposal of marriage;

are all situations into which I have been forced or led by circumstances from time to time, but from which I have tended by degrees to run away more and more.

There are inconsistencies, of course, in the view of those who are not

Yvonne Gregory

John Gielgud as Richard of Bordeaux, 1933

Maurice Goldberg

Laurence Olivier (the Ronald Colman phase), 1935

Gladys Cooper with the Author in *Excelsior*, 1928

in the position to understand the degrees and subtle shades of this complaint. People have found it difficult to see how I, its victim, was able to live in the restricted quarters of a one-roomed flat for twenty-five years. And why I, who had ceased in the end to be able to commit myself to work in the theatre, have always been happy in a B.B.C. studio, which is thickly padded and has no windows.

The answer is that I am able *of my own volition* at any moment to walk out of the flat into the street or out of a studio into the passage; and that the locks on the doors of broadcasting studios are always in perfect order and that there is usually a second exit anyway. Most important of all, a radio engagement is only for a few days; so I feel relatively uncommitted. I know I am going to be free again in a day or two's time. I can see daylight and the end of the tunnel. With a successful theatre play, as with *The Silver Cord*, you know you may be there, with two matinées a week, for months and months, or in the case of *The Mousetrap* for years and years, with perhaps a provincial tour at the end of it.

As to my difficulties about staying away in strange houses: one friend only, Nan Morrell, an R.A.D.A. colleague, showed her complete grasp of this complication; with the result that I enjoyed being several times with her and Margaret Whiting at Lyford Grange, near Wantage. Nan said to me, "You can keep the car in the drive outside the front door. If, even in the middle of the night, you feel you want to go home, you can go. And you needn't even leave a note behind to explain why."

This is true friendship and true understanding.

Now, after this—I think necessary—digression, I want to return to writing something about a humble theatre, one which was raised in status for a considerable period around this time, and about an actor whom I first saw playing there.

The Regent Theatre, King's Cross, which started life as a music-hall known as the Euston Theatre of Varieties, was in the 1920's to know great respectability and to be the scene of many noteworthy theatrical occasions, before becoming the cinema that it is today. Many actors were to appear on that stage at the Regent whose names are well known to us now in theatre, radio, films and television.

Back in the first part of the century, the Euston Theatre of Varieties had been a very different place. You could go to the Euston and see first-class "turns" like Marie Lloyd and your seat in the gallery would cost you twopence. It was the custom, I was once told by a local character, to take with you in a piece of newspaper "'alfpenny and a

c

'a'porth''. This meant a halfpennyworth of fried fish and a halfpenny-worth of chips; and in your pocket you carried a packet of Woodbines, which were five for a penny, ten for twopence.

But I did not carry with me any such delights on the afternoon when I went to a matinée at the Euston. Nor did I sit in the gallery for two-pence. I sat in the stalls for nothing. The Euston Theatre of Varieties by that time had become the Regent Theatre and managers realised then the importance of actors seeing plays and other actors' work, and were generous and hospitable with their complimentary seats. (Would that this custom could be revived.)

The play I saw that day was *Robert E. Lee* by John Drinkwater and the afternoon began with a disappointment. When we got into our seats we found in the programme a slip to the effect that Claude Rains was ill and was not appearing. I did not even notice the unknown understudy's name. But the unknown understudy himself, when he appeared, could not have escaped the notice of any member of that audience. Disappointment was short-lived; for we were aware that we were seeing in his performance something very special indeed. The force of his personality, the beauty of his voice, and a strange emana-tion of emotional power, all combined to turn the occasion into one of those rare theatre experiences that are never forgotten.

I went round afterwards to see a friend (Tristan Rawson) and I enquired the name of this unknown understudy. "A difficult name," he said, groping for it; "something like Gullgood. No—ah! Yes! Gielgud. That's it—John Gielgud."

On my way out I ran into the unknown understudy with the difficult name and was able to thank him for the pleasure he had given us. I did not know then that his exceptional talent was a precious gift handed down to him, on his mother's side, from the Terry family; nor could I foresee how much his name was going to mean to all who love the theatre in the times that were to come. Nor especially that I myself would owe entirely to him a new understanding and appreciation of Shakespeare. With my intellectual laziness, my Philistine upbringing and the usual academic approach at school to Shakespeare's plays, I tended to avoid them for many years. The little Shakespearean acting I did see was not of the kind that would make me want to see more. But when I saw John Gielgud's *Hamlet* a whole unknown world of poetry and beauty, allied to crystal-clear understanding, opened up before me. I have missed very few of Gielgud's Shakespearean performances since then, and very few Hamlets, for *Hamlet* became at that moment, and has remained, my favourite play.

I acted only once with Gielgud, in *Sons and Fathers* by Alan Monk-house, for a special occasion. John was then a very young man. His performance of a part in which he ended up as a grandfather, and his facility in slipping with complete ease from one generation to another were remarkable.

Of all the early work he did, his *Richard of Bordeaux* and his *Hamlet* at the New Theatre stand out most strongly in my memory. His *Macbeth* at the Piccadilly during the war I thought very fine indeed; and a wonderful example of his exceptional gift for mounting vocally, never seeming to over-reach himself, always appearing to have something in reserve. But if the clock could be put back, and I were allowed to choose a performance of Gielgud's to see again, I should unhesitatingly ask for the Prince of Denmark. Of this 1934 *Hamlet* Herbert Farjeon wrote:

"It is a long time since a London auditorium has been enlivened by such loud cheers as greeted Mr. John Gielgud last week after his first performance as Hamlet at the New Theatre. Probably there is no actor now on our stage, possibly there is no actress, with a following so large, enthusiastic and uncritical. It is comforting, therefore, to reflect that, unlike many popularities, Mr. Gielgud is an actor of fine taste and great ambition who needs must act the highest when he sees it, and that he is not likely to lead his supporters, as he so easily could, astray.

Mr. Gielgud's Hamlet is, by general consent, the best Hamlet seen since the war. It is a romantic not a classical Hamlet, a Hamlet bitter with the saltness of tears he does not shed, a Hamlet passing all his predecessors in adoration of his dead father. I have never seen this intense father-worship more beautifully emphasized than it is by Mr. Gielgud at the start of the play—rightly emphasized, for the text demands it, and the poignancy of Hamlet's failure to avenge his father in more than words is tremendously enhanced."

John Gielgud is never content. All through a run he watches himself with critical dispassion, paring things down, striving always to *simplify*: a word which I have heard him often use.

In his book, *Early Stages*, John writes of the toy theatres he used to play with in his childhood. I think it is true to say of Gielgud that he is still the boy he wrote of in that book: the boy with the toy theatre. All the hard work he has done and all that he has contributed to the drama in this country and abroad has only intensified those early enthusiasms and ideals. The child is single-minded about things, and John has never lost single-mindedness. The theatre was his first love and will hold his devotion to the end. He is one of those rare people on the stage who loves the theatre more than himself as an actor, and he would not be happy long away from that *milieu*. John Gielgud did once ask me to act with him after he had become famous. He was to play Obey's *Noah*, with Michel St. Denis directing it. They wanted me to take the part of Shem. Although important in the Biblical story, as a rôle I felt I could make little of it. Apart from this, I was not yet fully converted to what "theatre" really means. When I found myself, dressed up to the nines, on the stage of the New Theatre, with John and with St. Denis, businesslike and unsocial, in command; and when I saw a young man with flaming red hair and bright blue eyes, dressed in nothing but a pair of shorts (his name was Marius Goring) I was terrified. It was all so new to me, that sort of "set-up", as I should have called it then. I felt like a fish out of water and the fish took fright and wriggled off the hook. I think Gielgud was a little offended with me for a time, but long after *Noah* was over we corresponded and he forgave me, I know.

Although I only acted with John Gielgud on that one occasion I have mentioned, it will be seen that as a director he was to play an important part in the last years of the theatre phase of my life. This is a fragment of a letter he wrote to me after I had finally left the stage:

> . . . the countless friends and admirers who love you and your work will always regret your absence on our side of the footlights, where we all feel you rightly belong. You could still write and teach and yet act too, you know.
>
> Yours ever,
> John

It is not my intention to keep to any strict chronology in the writing of this book. In order of time the first sight of John Gielgud at the Regent Theatre came before *The Silver Cord*, very early in the 1920's.

So also did my first meeting with a man of letters who was beginning to play such a powerful rôle in the careers of many actors, actresses and playwrights, and whose weekly articles were eagerly read by the general newspaper public. By the time I met him James Agate must have been doing his column in *The Sunday Times* for about five years.

He was not only the most witty and entertaining dramatic critic in my memory, but his work was founded on a great knowledge of the theatre from years of enthusiastic theatre-going and on deep and wide reading of all that related to the history of acting, playwriting and dramatic criticism. Agate himself once said to me, mentioning two of his fellow critics: "I'm the best living writer on the theatre. A. writes better than I do, but wouldn't know an actor if he saw one. B. knows the hell of a lot about the theatre, but he can't write."

My first encounter with James Agate came about through Bernard Mortlock, an old family friend: Canon C. B. Mortlock, as he is now, Rector of St. Vedast in the City and Canon of Chichester. Amongst his many other activities he was doing the dramatic criticism for the *Church Times* and was present in his professional capacity on one of my important first nights. In the interval he sent me round a note, asking me if I could go out to supper with him after the show to meet James Agate.

Bernard took me to Romano's, where Agate soon joined us. My youthful nervousness in meeting so distinguished a man was greatly reduced by the fact that Agate arrived in the grip of a violent attack of asthma. This was an affliction with which I was particularly able to be sympathetic; it ran in my family and my father himself had suffered cruelly from it. I asked Agate if he had ever heard of a patent alleviator called Tucker's Atomiser. But asthma varies in its causes and cures, and J.A. told me he had already tried this remedy in vain.

I recollect little about that supper in the restaurant that had seen such romantic days. But I do remember Agate saying I ought to play some Shakespeare, and my replying that I felt unsuited to that sort of work. I was conscious then, as I still am, that my voice is not a good instrument for romantic or lyrical verse. (I had not at that time discovered that I could give a good account of myself in the prose parts such as Aguecheek or Trinculo, Launce or Launcelot Gobbo.) With my self-criticism Agate was presently to agree, when I was persuaded, much against my better judgment, to play the dark-eyed, romantic Lorenzo in *The Merchant of Venice*.

"... But I pounce with pleasure on Mr. Denys Blakelock's Lorenzo, since here is an admirable actor whose intellectuality in modern plays I have praised unendingly and almost to the point of incurring a charge of partiality. Let me then say with zest and without hesitation that his Lorenzo is the worst Shakespearean performance I have ever seen."

So J.A. was to write in the early 'Thirties; and no one realised more than I did the justice of this castigation. In fairness to myself, I must state that I did everything in my power to extricate myself from the engagement, both when I first had the offer and during the rehearsal period. I knew what was coming to me.

But that night at Romano's, Lorenzo lay far away in the future; and about two o'clock I went back happily to bed, grateful for the events of the evening, and looking no further forward than the following week-end, in hopeful anticipation of what my father used to call a "bit of fat" in *The Sunday Times*.

James Agate, like his successor Harold Hobson, was a Francophile. He was endlessly fascinated by the French theatre and by the subject of Sarah Bernhardt, with whom his actress sister, May Agate, had once studied. There seemed to be few of his articles that did not contain some reference to things French. Noël Coward is said to have remarked: "Nice man, Jimmie Agate—a pity he took that day trip to Boulogne."

There happened to be one French actress in whom I have for many years been especially interested—Eve Lavallière. I have already mentioned her in connection with *Le Roi*, the adaptation of which, *The Royal Visitor*, I had played in. She had been a celebrated figure in the theatre world of Paris, and was at the height of her fame during the reign of Edward VII. Lavallière was almost "royal" herself.* "Male Royalties, passing through Paris, were delighted to meet her. Edward VII, Alfonso XIII, King Manoel of Portugal and Prince Henry of Bavaria, being only a few of the notabilities who sought to pay their homage in person. She kept a sumptuous flat, first in the *rue Rivoli* and later in the *Champs Elysées*, and her furnishing and interior decoration schemes were the *dernier cri* among the smart set of the Parisian theatre world."

But a day came, many years later, when she turned from all this. Through the influence of a simple curé in the country, where she had gone to study her rôles for a world tour with Lucien Guitry, she was reconciled to the Catholic Faith of her birth. She there and then gave up everything, paying large sums to be released from her contract with Guitry Père. She became a member of the Third Order of St. Francis, living a wonderful life of prayer, self-denial and charitable works, until she died in 1929.

I wrote enquiringly about her to James Agate. This was his reply:

22, Antrim Mansions, 1st December, 1936
Dear Denys Blakelock,
        I am afraid I don't know anything about Lavallière except that she

* Adapted from *A Modern Magdalen* by L. L. McReavy.

squinted. Whether she was a good actress or not I can't say. With the exception of Sarah and Réjane I have never seen any French actress who wasn't exactly like any other. I wish I could help you.

Now will you please do something for me? This is to apologise to your father for not answering his letter. But I have only just re-discovered your address and have been terribly busy, as various of my recently published tomes will prove.

If he will now repeat his kindness and make a definite date I will do my utmost to keep it.

Yours,

James Agate

I do not believe Lavallière squinted. Alex Scott-Gatty described a meeting with her during the first war, "in the house of the mistress of a wealthy bookmaker in Curzon Street". He particularly mentioned her great dark eyes, which are plainly without so much as a cast in all the photographs I have seen of her. But it must be remembered that Lavallière was a light-comedy actress and French tragediennes were Agate's great passion. Moreover, he was not a religious man and the Catholic element and Eve Lavallière's renunciation would not, I am sure, have appealed to him at all.

I also think this was an example of an "impish" streak in Agate. He enjoyed saying things that shocked and surprised. When he was writing film criticisms he told me of a gushing lady who said to him:

"Oh, Mr. Agate, I did so agree with your opinion of that film at the Plaza."

"I didn't see it," Agate replied.

"But you wrote an article about it in the Tatler."

"I didn't see *that* either."

And he hadn't. I believe it was written by Jock (Alan) Dent, a great friend and one who could write in exact imitation of Agate's style.

He made another confession to me one day, when I asked him how he found the time to write the weekly book reviews in a daily paper. "My dear boy," he said, "you don't think I *read* them, do you?" He went on to explain that he had only to look at the beginning, glance at the end and read a chunk in the middle to be able to write intelligently about a book.

At that time I had done no writing myself and was insufficiently shocked by this bland admittance. Had I then realised something of the headache and heartache and the infinite pains that go to the making of an author's finished work, I should have been less amused.

But that was James Agate. He was in demand in every direction and no doubt found it difficult to refuse the offers made to him; particularly as he spent wildly and was always in need of the money they brought.

The second part of his letter about Lavallière helped to precipitate Agate's visit to my home. He had mentioned it as a possibility in an entry in one of his *Egos*:

"*Thursday: May 30*
Took Denys Blakelock to supper. He confessed to a *bon mot* at my expense. Asked whether I was going to the first night of 'Acropolis', he had said, 'Sure. I met him this afternoon, coming away from his crammers!!'
Promises to invite me home to lunch with his people as soon as I can satisfy him that I am 'Vicarage-trained'."

I never thought it would actually take place, but it did. Of this visit he wrote afterwards in *Ego 3* as follows:

"To passing a jolly Sunday evening at the home of Denys Blakelock's father, who has built three churches on the same spot—first a wooden shanty, replaced by a tin building, and now by a noble edifice of brick. A large-minded Church of England clergyman who lives in amity with two sons who have gone over to the Roman Catholic faith. The Vicar told me how Muswell Hill was made by the murderers Milsom and Fowler. Thousands flocked to the scene of the crime and among them speculators who spotted something doing in the building line. Among the first erections was the little wooden church. . . . There was a delicious supper of the cold beef order—no kickshaws—and after the Vicar had gone to bed we (being Denys, his brother Alban, and Alban's wife and myself) sat up late talking our best metaphysics."

I well remember that talk about religion and J.A. saying he found it difficult to believe that God, at a particular point in time, came down from Heaven and took upon Himself human flesh and human personality, and dwelt among His creatures. That evening left me with the general impression that James Agate was one of those who believed in nothing beyond this life, but deep down in his heart would have given much to be able to do so. One or two things I heard in after years made me revise this opinion. Agate had been brought up as a Unitarian; and belief in only one Person of the Godhead would account for his difficulty in accepting the Incarnation of God the Son.

I shall always think of his many kindnesses with gratitude. The last letter I received from him was written only a few weeks before he died, in answer to one from me concerning a book I was then writing.

Tem. Bar 8965   Queen Alexandra Mansions,
(when it works)   Grape Street, W.C.2.
                                 March 29, '47

Dear Denys,

Anything you like. Anything I have written about you, or said to or about you, is entirely at your service. If you like I will go through my records and copy out anything relevant.

I am a great admirer of yours, and in Hamlet's words, "loved you ever" . . .

Why not come to lunch, and then adjourn to my flat where you can look anything up?

Am in the middle, and I hope threequarters through a breakdown owing to too much work, too much play and too much drink.

Come and hold my hand, in the nicest way of course. Have been quite seriously ill. Let me hear from you.

                         Ever,
                         Jimmie

This letter was typical of Agate. Busy and unwell though he might be, he was prompt to offer help of a practical kind.

Some weeks later I went to lunch with him. He seemed well on the road to recovery that afternoon, when I saw him into his taxi outside the Ivy. It is my last memory of him. He died soon after that.

I went to his memorial service at St. Martin-in-the-Fields, where he and I had sat together at the service to Henry Ainley not so very long before.

CHAPTER XIII

Spread Eagle   New Theatre, June, 1928

"Denys Blakelock, as the boy who is sent to his death as a bait to bring about Government intervention in Mexico, gives his best performance up to now."

I T W A S N O T my best performance; only the biggest and most important part I had yet been given. Oh, this inability to distinguish between the actor and his part; between the actor with the opportunity and the actor without one.

The play would have been a success, I am certain, if it had been done some years later. But in 1928 audiences were much less familiar with the American outlook and American terminology and slang; and the play, despite the presence of Raymond Massey in the cast and a good Press, only ran a short time. However, it proved to be a good stepping-stone for me.

H. M. Harwood had something to do with the script of *Spread Eagle*; and it was he who suggested me to Gladys Cooper for the boy in her autumn production at the Playhouse. She had only seen me in the *Spring Cleaning* part, and was doubtful as to my suitability to play her "true love". However, she came to see *Spread Eagle* and changed her mind.

The next morning found me driving up to London on my way to the Playhouse where they were already rehearsing. I could hardly believe that I was actually going to play an intimate scene with this untouchable Goddess whom I had worshipped at a distance for so many years. My great fear was that I might lose the part through lack of inches, as Gladys Cooper had always appeared to me to be rather tall. So into my shoes I had put some elevators as a precaution, but by the time I got to London they were so uncomfortable that I was forced to jettison them by the road-side. I need have had no fear. When I came to stand by Gladys Cooper I found her less tall than I had imagined; and in the first scene, when the height question mattered most, she wore flat-heeled slippers, and that difficulty was smoothed away. Without high heels she was well below me in height.

How lovely she looked during those rehearsals! She had had a long rest and had just returned from a holiday in Switzerland. Her golden hair, her delicately sun-tanned skin, and those enormous blue eyes set so perfectly in relation to the nose were something to remember for ever. I was never disillusioned by meeting Gladys Cooper. She has always remained glamorous to me, and of her beauty one could never tire.

I was a little in awe of her during that first engagement; but I soon discovered that, as with all people in her position, she liked to be treated as a human being and not as a celebrity. She liked to talk about her house and garden, her home life and of course about her children. The maternal element in her was strong, and her acting at its best when that side of her nature was brought into play. I remember her telling me that she had refused to see *The Silver Cord*. One could well understand that to such a healthy-minded woman the psychologically involved theme of that play about maternal love would be repugnant.

Gladys Cooper was very easy to act with—generous and unselfish with everyone. But she discovered that I was given to stage hysteria and she tried me hard. This did not matter in the first scene, where she had to push me backwards on to a table and tickle me, when we could both take advantage of the stage directions. But in the other two scenes I was supposed to be angry with her; and Gladys's blue eyes, bubbling over with merriment, were again and again too much for my self-control. This hysteria on the stage was always from my student days a serious problem. I am not referring to that worst form of bad manners, private joking between the actors, which rightly infuriates an audience when they spot it; but to the genuine nervous desire to laugh for no reason whatever, which assails you most at those moments when you are required to be especially serious.

In this particular weakness I was not helped by having Hermione Baddeley in the cast. Not only was she herself a victim to the complaint, but I only had to take one look at the irresistibly amusing face of that comic genius to begin to break up. In the end we played our scene together avoiding each other's eyes. This was a pity. When you begin to resort to devices of that kind to combat stage hysteria it harms your work. There is only one answer to this, as to all, weaknesses; to face up to it and look your fellow actor straight in the eye.

The play of which I am now writing was called *Excelsior*, and was an adaptation from *L'Ecole des Cocottes*. Gladys Cooper had tried it out at a Sunday performance, when John Gielgud had played the part that was afterwards entrusted to me. In his book, *Early Stages*, he mentions this production and is kind enough to say that I was better in the piece than he had been. But that is only Gielgud's characteristic generosity.

The fact is that Robert in *Excelsior* had suffered considerably in translation from the French; I was mediocre in a thankless part, which John must have been glad that another engagement prevented him from playing.

Round about this time, when I struck a spate of these unsatisfactory rôles, I remember one of my more candid friends telling me that he overheard someone in a theatre-bar saying, "What a pity Denys Blakelock has gone off so, as an actor."

A golden rule for success in the theatre, I am sure, is: never accept a bad part if you can afford to wait for a good one. Nothing succeeds like success; but nothing can fail more successfully than a performance that fails to succeed.

However, I had acted with Gladys Cooper; and that was an experience I had never expected to have in those days when I had sent her postcard photographs to sign and had stood waiting to see her outside that same stage-door that I was now using as a matter of course. Gladys Cooper is an interesting and rather admirable character. She is honest, forthright, strong-minded and courageous. Like so many beautiful women she is completely lacking in vanity. She takes her looks for granted. She has had a great many troubles in her life and has taken them in her stride, remaining up to this present moment of her seventies an industrious and highly successful actress.

She tells a story about herself which illustrates her independent character. Once, as a young chorus girl, she was riding in a bus and she saw one of the "kept" Gaiety actresses bowling down the Bayswater Road in her carriage, wrapped in her rich furs. "Yes," thought Gladys Cooper, "I'm going to have those one day. But I'm going to pay for them myself."

CHAPTER XIV

THE HECTIC 'TWENTIES dissolved almost unnoticed into the quieter 'Thirties. The Bright Young Things became less bright as they went deeper into the next decade. They began to realise that peace in our time was more easily talked about than made secure. New Ideologies began to spring up and certain names took on a sinister sound. Passing through Germany, I saw HITLER in large black letters on a hoarding and wondered idly who he was. There were faint rumbles of thunder in the far distance, which became ominously less faint as each year went by. This was the background against which we lived our lives. The theatre went on as usual.

My own personal life had taken a less happy turn. The *Eric or Little by Little* of the *Spring Cleaning* days had long ago gone down the wind; and the process of a belated growing-up proved a protracted and painful experience.

On the professional side, John Gielgud expressed my predicament very well in this paragraph of a letter he once wrote to me:

"... And you convey most truthfully how the youthful exhibitionism, which lends one confidence as a stage-struck beginner, develops with alarming suddenness into an almost pathological doubt of one's potential talents just at the very moment when one first achieves success."

I myself was feeling this doubt of my own abilities very strongly at that period. The showy, easy acting opportunities of the early days came my way less and less frequently. And because I had always run away from the difficult things and had not really worked as a student, I found myself lost and timorous when the more ambitious things were offered to me.

So my career as an actor went forward fitfully. Sometimes it would climb a small peak, only to drop soon again to the level slopes. It is strange, looking back, to find how few plays there were in which I was concerned that were of any enduring value to the theatre history books; and yet many of them seemed to have an importance at the time.

One of the few of real distinction that comes to my mind immediately is Pirandello's *Henry IV*, known here as *The Mock Emperor*. The play itself is a classic and is bound to appear on the theatrical scene from time to time. Of recent years Paul Scofield has done it on sound radio and Albert Finney on the stage at the Citizens', Glasgow.

But its first showing in London will always be associated with a great actor whose name I have not yet mentioned, as we did not meet professionally until he asked me to play the Marquis di Nolli in the Pirandello play. I am referring to Ernest Milton and I do not use the word "great" lightly.

Milton's performance in the title rôle was magnificent. I think he was the one actor who could play that tragic king as it had to be played. Ernest's exceptional powers demand exceptional parts—strong or strange ones. When he finds them he seems to consume and recreate himself emotionally within the rôle, dying like the phoenix, as it were, in order to live again. In *The Mock Emperor* Pirandello had supplied the immortal fire; and generous as Ernest was to those who acted with him his performance alone stands out in the memory. Here, in Graham Robertson's *Letters*, is an eye-witness of the first night:

"I was thrilled as I had never hoped again to be in a theatre. Ernest is superb from his first entrance, when the immense dignity of the fantastic figure with painted cheeks hushes the house with dead silence, to the last wonderful moment when it sits lonely upon its high throne staring out into eternity. It's a marvellous performance, full of the finest artistry and of the highest imagination. I have seen nothing like it since Irving."

Amongst the theatrical events I missed, to my regret and shame, was Ernest Milton's Hamlet. There is no doubt that it must have been something quite exceptional, for so often one comes upon mention of it in one direction or another. Only the other day (also in Graham Robertson's *Letters*) I read, "If ever you get the chance of seeing Milton's Hamlet *rush* to it." And again, "I certainly like him better than most Hamlets including Johnston (Forbes Robertson) . . . Milton is romantic and Rossettian on the Irving lines. His 'Rogue and peasant slave' speech is electrifying and unforgettable."

A much younger man, John Clements, found him unforgettable too. When asked on the radio what was the greatest single stage perfor-mance he remembered Clements replied, "Ernest Milton's Hamlet". And Alec Guinness, in his theatre book, wrote that he had seen eight or nine Hamlets of which Milton's was the best.

The performance of which Clements spoke was the 1934 Sadlers Wells *Hamlet* in its entirety, with Sybil Thorndike as the Queen.

Milton played the part several times, but it was his second Hamlet at the Old Vic in 1922 which attracted the attention of the brilliant editor, critic and novelist, Naomi Royde-Smith, who was an influential figure of that period. She was Problems Editor and Poetry Editor on the *Westminster Gazette* in which she published two first poems: one by Rupert Brooke, the other by a young man not now associated with poetry, Graham Greene. She was also the dramatic critic, and had for her second string a new writer called Aldous Huxley, who was followed later by a young Mr. A. P. Herbert.

Naomi Royde-Smith told me that one day she noticed, lying in the office wastepaper basket, some discarded theatre tickets. She was informed that they were for something that would not interest her: "Only the Old Vic," they said. She picked them out, however, and insisted on going to the play. They were giving a performance of *King John* that night and she was immediately impressed by the magnetism and artistry of the actor who played the King—Ernest Milton.

After that Naomi Royde-Smith became a regular visitor to the Old Vic, taking with her many important people in the literary world, including, I remember her telling me, Walter de la Mare. There is no doubt that her patronage of the Old Vic in its early days under Lilian Baylis and the tremendous spread she gave to Milton's Hamlet, and to his other performances too, in the *Westminster Gazette*, were greatly responsible for swelling the excited audiences that flocked to the Waterloo Road night after night and who developed into the Old Vic's faithful public.

The dramatic critic became *persona grata* there and met many of the players back-stage—including the leading man. At one of her literary parties later on one guest said to another: "Who is that bird of paradise Naomi's got hold of?" It was Ernest Milton. Three years after that they were married.

I once talked to Milton about verse-speaking of which he is a master. He told me that he had no tuition in this art but he had had his singing voice trained and was therefore "familiar with the ictus". His years of hard work at the Old Vic did the rest.

John Gielgud, also, denied that he had had any special instruction in speaking verse. He said he felt "rather ashamed" that he could not point back to something particular of that kind in his early days. I hardly think Sir John need feel any such regret, when one sees the results in him today.

I was not altogether surprised at his and Milton's answers to my enquiry. They bore out a theory of mine about this important branch of dramatic art. I believe that actors are divided into two kinds: those that can speak verse and those that cannot. That the instinct for this art is something inborn, and that, although it would be a mistake to underrate the value of tuition in the technique of verse-speaking, all the training in the world is of little use if you do not have it in you from the beginning; and that there are many first-rank speakers of verse, who, because they have this inborn instinct, make great reputations for themselves without technical training.

Then again, there is the voice itself. Not everyone can have a beautiful voice, such as Robert Donat had for instance. That is a gift all too rare. But for Shakespeare and the Greek tragedies one does need a voice that has a fullness, a richness, a physical robustness not called upon for modern speech. As I have said, my own voice is singularly unsuited to the classical medium when it comes to the poetic passages. Hence my failure in *The Merchant of Venice*: a minor disaster for me, a major triumph for Milton, under whose management the play was presented. His Shylock was another of his great creations, dignified, touching and beautifully spoken.

On the Monday evening following James Agate's notice of my Lorenzo in *The Sunday Times,* I ran into Milton outside the theatre and offered him my resignation. He would not hear of it. Many actor-managers in those circumstances might well have seized upon the chance I gave him. But Ernest was always generous and kind to the artists in his employ and he was determined to stand by the faith he had put in me. Even more generous, perhaps, was my *vis à vis,* Lydia Sherwood, whose beauty and musical cadences made her the perfect Jessica. She never by the flick of an eyelash betrayed the agony it must have been to be saddled with a Lorenzo so inadequate, so ill-matched.

After the finish of that run I never acted in the theatre with Milton again; although we met in a television production of *The Mock Emperor* and in a radio version of another great success of his, *Loyalties* by John Galsworthy.

I saw him once in a part quite different from any other I had seen him play. It was a modern piece, *Rope,* by Patrick Hamilton, and his rôle gave him the opportunity to display his gift for sophisticated comedy. He was very funny indeed. I for ever afterwards wondered why stage producers have made so little use of that side of Ernest Milton's work, and have failed to capitalise for comedic purposes this actor's inimitable voice and personality.

Although I had made several unsuccessful attempts to break away on my own, by 1930 I had finally settled down into living with my family in my father's large North London vicarage overlooking the Alexandra Palace, which was to become the first home of television. But it was in 1930 that the first big change in our lives took place with the death of my mother.

It was lovely summer weather, I remember, which only served to accentuate more sharply that feeling of unreality and sadness, which descends upon a household when one knows for certain that the end is near. On that last day, as my mother was unconscious and I could do nothing, I went over to Kenwood to lunch with Aubrey Ensor who was then custodian. The beauty of the house, of the ancient trees and smooth, sloping lawns is inseparable in my memory from the events of that hot August afternoon. In the evening I had to work, as I was in a play at the Everyman Theatre in Hampstead. An hour or two after I reached home my mother died. People think it brave that actors continue to carry on in such circumstances. But in fact it is a very great help to be working when these bereavements come upon us. From that time onwards we all three, my brother and his wife, Alban and Renée, and I kept my father company at home. We have always been very much in one another's lives ever since.

But eight years later the death of my father, too, brought an end to that background of deceptive security. It was the complete break-up at last of the old settled way of life: a life free of all responsibility, all anxiety in regard to ways and means and the practical considerations of running a home. Three months after that we moved into a flat in Woburn Square and we remained in the Bloomsbury district for twenty-five years. Having endured the tedious journey to and from North London for so long, it was a relief to be within walking distance of the theatres and the B.B.C. But ironically enough, Alban and I found ourselves frequently on our way back to North London. Television had begun at the Alexandra Palace, which had such associations with our childhood days, and we both appeared in some of the earliest plays that were done on that medium.

One small episode in that connection is worth recalling, for the light it throws on the difference between the inconsequential conditions of programme planning as it was then from what we now take for granted in the *Radio Times*.

My brother played Henry VIII in a one-act play, presented on that postage stamp-sized screen for a single afternoon performance. It was a success; and no less a personage than the Head of Television said to him afterwards: "Are you free this evening? Would you feel like doing it for us again tonight?"

Many years previously we had both cashed in on the start of sound radio. The premises were on Savoy Hill and crystal sets and headphones were in use at the receiving end. Everything was very smart in those pioneer times. We all put on our best clothes, especially for the transmissions. There was no machinery for prerecording, so that everything went out "live". Announcers wore dinner-jackets and it was quite usual to see many of the cast in evening dress.

It was most unnatural in me as an actor, and doubtless pathological and deeply suspect, that I ultimately preferred radio drama to any other medium. As a child I had been told that "little boys should be seen and not heard". Perhaps it is a perversity in me that I now prefer to be *heard and not seen*.

CHAPTER XV

One late afternoon in the summer of 1933 a clergyman climbed the steep setts up to Haworth Parsonage and rang the bell twice at the Brontës old home. After a time and unwillingly it was answered by the curator himself. The visitor was too late; the museum was closed.

"But I have travelled many miles," he cried, "and my son is acting the part of Branwell in *The Brontës* at the Royalty Theatre in London."

From that year of 1933 onwards a rash of Brontë plays spread itself over the face of London's theatre and the one to get in first was Alfred Sangster's, called *The Brontës*, in which I played Branwell: "the Rector's son! A profligate, a drunkard!"—as Charlotte herself described him.

Shortly after that my father was to have another son in a second Brontë play. My brother, Alban, was in *Wild Decembers* by Clemence Dane. Our version was simple, unpretentious and convincing. The other was impressive, distinguished, but vaguely literary in style, lacking the stuff of life which ours seemed to have. We ran from April on into the late autumn; they opened long after we did and closed in about six weeks.

Lydia Sherwood in *The Brontës* damped down her exceptional attractions to bring to Charlotte reality and perfect truth; Diana Wynyard in *Wild Decembers* was persuaded to bring all her beauty into play, which made her Charlotte a disappointment. Beatrix Lehmann's startling intellectuality somehow failed to wipe out from the critics' minds the recent picture Dorothy Black had presented of Emily. Her dark, romantic looks, her deep and tragic tones exactly fitted the popular image of the author of *Wuthering Heights*. A lesser rôle of Nicholls, the curate who married Charlotte, was played by the still young Ralph Richardson, with that special compelling quality of his own that makes him spring to mind immediately after all these years.

The Branwell in *Wild Decembers* was Emlyn Williams. How his performance compared with mine I do not know; the two parts were so completely different in their author's approach. I only know I enjoyed playing Branwell. He and I had so much in common. Did we not both stem from the same Victorian country-rectory background? And I did not find it difficult to enter into Branwell's melancholic temperament.

In *The Brontës* it was a short part but a very showy one, though spoiled by being all over at the beginning of the play. This is fatal from an actor's point-of-view. The critics and the audience have forgotten you by the time the evening is ended. On the other hand, in an actor's reckoning, a part that gives you a drunk scene with the family; and another, alone upon the stage, grovelling on the floor at night, drink-taken and drug-taking, gibbering in the moonlight streaming through the Parsonage windows; to end by being carried up to bed in father's arms—such a rôle is not to be despised. Even I did not despise Branwell.

I had another success in the 'Thirties. That also was at the Royalty, where Leon M. Lion produced a play called *The World of Light*. This was one of the most distinguished and provocative pieces of writing for the theatre of that decade. People often remind me of it still and say how stimulating they found it. This is no matter for surprise when one considers that its author was Aldous Huxley.

I always took for granted that Hugo, an introverted Cambridge don, the part I played, was based on Huxley himself. I was thirty at the time, exactly the age I was supposed to be; but I did not look it. This was for many years a disadvantage for me, that I was so light-weight in voice and personality and looked so much younger than I was. It troubled me particularly in *The World of Light*. Throughout rehearsals I felt that I was not giving the author what he wanted; though this seemed to be belied by the results when once we opened, and by the things he wrote to me in a letter which I proudly pasted into my copy of the play. I wish he could have said a few of them during the rehearsal period. He sat there in the darkness of the stalls, silent and as I thought disapproving. But he was a shy, remote man and I think he would have found it difficult to make contact with a company of actors.

My relationship with Leon M. Lion, as producer, was also a harrassing one. I owed my ultimate success to his perfectionist direction, I realised afterwards, but he worried me a great deal during rehearsals. He has the distinction of being the only producer who ever reduced me to drinking brandies and sodas in the middle of the morning.

For one recurring phrase alone I shall be for ever grateful to Lion. Over and over again he would stop me on a line and say, "Yes, but we don't *believe* you, dear boy". I have always remembered those words; they seem to me so exactly to hit the nail on the head as a test of reality in acting. It is fatally easy to learn words and speak them intelligently and make them sound acceptable, especially if they are well-written. But how often in the theatre one thinks to oneself, "Yes, but I don't believe that. It's only play-acting".

Of my performance in *The World of Light* a young gentleman up at Cambridge wrote the following in the *Granta*:

"Mr. Denys Blakelock's part was the sort that asks for a state of nervous tension rather than a technique."

I wonder where he got that idea?

We can smile indulgently at undergraduates, but we have to turn a respectful countenance towards the professional dramatic critic. He can play an influential part in the life of an actor. I think it is wise for us theatre people to decide early on how important that part is to be and to what extent we are going to allow dramatic criticism to influence us either way. It is easy to be unduly cast-down by a bad "notice", or disproportionately elated by a good one. By what I have written up to now I think I have shown that I have no grudge against dramatic critics. Some actors talk as if they were our natural enemies. Not this one. I have acknowledged a debt, for instance, to William Archer for a constructive criticism of my diction, which led to my taking special voice lessons. I have shown, too, that I had reason to be grateful to James Agate. I met, or came to know in one degree or another, many dramatic critics: W. A. Darlington, J. C. Trewin, Herbert Farjeon, St. John Ervine, Kenneth Tynan, Alan Dent and Collie Knox. In every case I found them kind and friendly in their attitude towards actors. So I cannot be accused of having any animus towards those from whose pens I have for the most part benefited. What I am trying to do now is to make an honest attempt to assess the value of professional dramatic criticism to the actor himself, as opposed to the theatregoer and the reader of newspapers.

To begin with it is quite plain that the critic can be of incalculable assistance to us from a careerist point-of-view. A crop of good Press notices can bring the agents to the telephone and the managers knocking on our door. To be a "critic's pet" and to get consistently favourable notices over a considerable period creates a general impression of success and helps to make and consolidate an actor's reputation. Perhaps that is why he tends to run a mile from dramatic critics, as I did for many years. I remember, at a first night party after *The Silver Cord*, scrupulously avoiding St. John Ervine, in whose play I had recently appeared, in terror lest he should think I was toadying for a mention in his *Observer* column.

So a leading actor's progress can be assured if he captures the fancy of the critics; and a supporting player be more constantly in work if he frequently finds favour in their regard. But from an artistic point of view? To what extent should an actor look to the professional critic for guidance in his creative work in the theatre? I think, for what my opinion is worth, to a very limited extent and for a multitude of reasons.

In one of a collection of letters from Granville Barker to John Gielgud, lent me by the latter, Barker says: "For a foundation of criticism technical knowledge is needed." I do not see how anyone can begin to criticise a performance constructively unless he knows something of the complications of the actor's art; the conditions under which he works; his dependence on the other artists he is acting with; and on the direction, for good or bad, of the producer, to whom he owes absolute obedience. The best a critic can do for an actor surely is to record the ultimate effect the performance has made on him. Most critics have to decide this very quickly and write it down at great speed to be in time for their papers.

Then again critics are human, and however well-intentioned they may be and however unquestionable their integrity, they must be subject to changing moods. I myself am an ardent playgoer; but I know only too well how difficult it is not to feel "agin" the play if it happens to catch you in the wrong mood. One does remember cases where a critic has paid a second visit and reversed his initial unfavourable verdict.

Then there is the bewildering conflict of opinions between people who are supposed to be experts writing on the same subject. One concrete example of this I can quote from my own experience when I was in *Lady Windermere's Fan*: Desmond Macarthy's unfavourable view of my "insufficiently elegant mode of speech"; as against Ivor Brown's statement in *The Observer* that "Mr. Denys Blakelock has the perfect delivery for this kind of thing."

I believe that dramatic critics are mainly for the theatre public and for theatre historians. As an actor there came a time when I decided to be glad and grateful when I had a good review; but not to be downcast if it were a bad one. And I looked for praise or blame first and foremost from my producer; and after that from those few informed friends and fellow-artists whose sincere opinions I knew that I could trust. One lesson I learned very early: never, *never* to write to a dramatic critic, either to thank him for a good notice or to admonish him for a bad. It is not our place to thank him for doing his job according to his conscience. And to find fault with him is fatal anyway. He always has the last word.

CHAPTER XVI

ONE FINE DAY in the summer of 1932 Ivor Novello asked me to go down to Redroofs, his home near Maidenhead. Sitting by the swimming-pool in the hot sun, he told me about a new comedy he had written. But the part turned out to be another *Spring Cleaning* young man; and, grateful though I was for the offer, I hesitated to break my resolution never to return to that sort of character. However, when the play came up for production I was without an engagement; and so decided to accept after all, when Ivor and Gladys Cooper, with whom he was going to do the play, offered me the part again. The prospect of working with two people whom I admired so much and whose united names gave a *cachet* to any production, was too much for me anyway. Moreover, I felt that by this time I was sufficiently well known in the theatre world to play another rôle of that kind without its doing me harm professionally. My optimism was justified. The engagement did me nothing but good; and the part proved to be very effective, with its witty and outrageous lines to which Ivor used to add delightedly during rehearsals. He even included some suggestions of my own.

Flies In The Sun was not one of Novello's best plays. There was something amiss with it and it did not run long. The story took place in the South of France amongst the sun-bathing "smart set" and their hangers-on. At least three of the characters were based on real people. The leading man played by Novello was supposed to be John Gilbert, the silent film-star, whose career had collapsed with the arrival of the talking picture. The inevitable Elsa Maxwell came into it; and Gladys Cooper's rôle was a picture of Daisy—The Hon. Mrs. Reggie-Fellowes, a good-looking, very rich woman and one of the leaders in the social circle of those days.

This was not a good part for Gladys. She had no amusing lines. In fact she had nothing to do but to look beautiful. That is not enough to hold an adoring audience with. Gladys Cooper could have done with more of the leading player's vanity that I have already mentioned. In her particular position she should have been careful to choose always characters extremely sympathetic to her large and special public.

Ivor Novello for once, in *Flies In The Sun*, had failed to bring his usual instinctive knowledge in such matters into play in the writing of his own part, as well as his leading lady's. Ivor's famous profile and

Gladys Cooper's beauty could not save *Flies In The Sun* from being a dull play.

As can often happen with a supporting player's part, I came off the best, as the chief hanger-on, with a good scene in each act packed with entertaining lines. It will come as no surprise to the reader who has read the earlier chapters of this book that my success in this part brought the usual trouble in its train: I immediately went down with severe influenza and was out of the cast for two weeks. This was not only sorrowful for me, but serious for the management. I have a picture postcard still, sent me by Gladys Cooper, on the back of which she had written:

"It's frightful how we miss you. Do come back soon—even if you have to play the sunbathing scene in a fur coat."

All this led to an episode which is worth mentioning, because it is such a good example of the humiliations to which actors are so frequently subjected. It is not easy for anyone in the theatrical profession to have a swollen head for long.

After my recovery I went one morning into my Bank at home, a little pleased with myself for once and enjoying my return to the limelight. The cashier across the counter said he was sorry I had been ill and asked, "What are you doing now?" I told him I was back at the theatre. "Oh," he said, "so they took you on again, then."

While *Flies In The Sun* was running Ivor Novello invited me down for a week-end to Redroofs. I had not by then set my face altogether against staying away; and in this case it was in circumstances of exceptional luxury and of glamour at first hand. We started off from the stage-door in the Rolls, Ivor turning on the inside light so that the crowd of waiting adorers could see him clearly. He was delightfully ingenuous in such matters and made no pretence of being too grand or blasé to give pleasure to his fans whom he looked upon as friends.

A new wing was being built on to Redroofs; and when we arrived about one o'clock Bobby Andrews and I were with Ivor when he saw the improvements for the first time. They consisted of a magnificent new bedroom, with a door opening on to an outside staircase that led down into the garden and to the swimming pool. His pleasure was quite childlike.

Ivor had all the endearing qualities: kindness and charm, a naturally sunny disposition, and an unquenchable enthusiasm for life. His own theatrical activities were legion, but he never missed any new play that was worth seeing. Just as John Gielgud has remained the boy with the toy theatre, so I think that Ivor Novello, who had so many thousands of fans to his credit, continued to the end to be the young Welsh boy who once stood, he told me, outside Daly's stage door to get a glimpse of Lily Elsie.

When I was at the Playhouse with the Novello play I used to do some imitations, the best of which was one of Noël Coward. Gladys Cooper thought well of it and when Coward came to see the show she made me do it to his face. This embarrassed me and so no doubt it did Noël Coward, though he passed it off with his usual aplomb. But that imitation was to prove of great use to me in the very near future, in the building up of a difficult part.

In the late autumn of 1933 a play arrived from across the Atlantic by one of America's most distinguished playwrights, Robert Emett Sherwood. Marc Connelly, author of *Green Pastures*, was to direct it and the large cast was full of either stars or of actors of reputation.

The play was called *Acropolis* and many of the names that we associate with ancient Athens were to be found amongst the *dramatis personae*: names such as Pheidias, Alcibiades, Socrates, and Aspasia, played by Gladys Cooper. It was Aristophanes that fell to me and I was told from the beginning to think of him as an Athenian Noël Coward. It was then that I hit on the idea of utilising my imitation. As the dialogue was written in the modern idiom it seemed to fit quite well, when I used Coward's quick, staccato, "plummy" way of speaking. Exactly how good my imitation was is doubtful. Only one person from the front ever mentioned it. But it did help me to get the "feel" of the character, which was not an easy one to come to terms with.

As in the case of *The Royal Visitor*, the play was a costly failure, though a more distinguished one. We seemed to rehearse for weeks and we ran for one. The American backer lost £8,000.

After the first night I was asked to a small supper party at the Savoy. I was interested to meet Hugh Walpole whose novels I had admired. He told me that the Polchester in his books is a composite picture of two Cathedral towns. I was much more than just interested to meet Epstein, a friendly, humorous man. When I asked him what he thought of our expensive Grecian décor he said significantly, "Alma Tadema!".

CHAPTER XVII

To RESORT, AS I did in *Acropolis*, to imitating a real person is not a practice to encourage; as the best kind of acting is impersonation, interior identification and not imitation. It should come from within outwards and not be superimposed from outside. Yet one cannot deny that sometimes one is forced to employ this method; and the end justifies the means if it comes off. In a children's play, Eleanor Farjeon's *The Silver Curlew* that belongs to a much later date than this, I was rehearsing the part of King Nollekens, a cry-baby King who went about with his Nanny. The part was beautifully written; I was right for the part; the point of identification was all but reached. But there was something missing. I saw at last that it was my walk that was wrong. I was speaking and moving in the manner of a small boy, but I was taking the long strides of a grown-up man. So I began to rehearse in a pair of light, indoor slippers and to take smaller steps. This immediately had its effect. From that moment onwards I became Nollekens and Nollekens became me.

I had a similar experience, this time again with speech, in James Bridie's play *The Black Eye*, presented by C. B. Cochran in 1935. I found the dialogue at first quite impossible to speak. The secret of it eluded me. It might well have been one of those many occasions in my career when the defeatist, diffident side of my nature forced me to resign the part and run away. But I soon saw that the lines were written essentially in the Scots idiom and called for Scottish cadences. H. K. Ayliff, the producer, decided that being the eldest of the large Windle-straw family I could justifiably speak with a slight accent. So I started again on fresh lines; and in the creation of this—for me—most difficult rôle I sought advice from many members of the big company. I soon gave that up. I found that all the English actors wanted to tell me how to talk Scots and all the Scottish actors to teach me how to act.

However, as often happens when we agonise over a part, it turned out rather well. The character suddenly emerged from within; and of the accent I became inordinately proud. But pride was soon to have its fall; for when Bridie arrived from the North he said that my accent must go. I had turned his Kelvinside Scottish gentleman into a dock-hand from the banks of the Clyde.

But when I cut out the accent entirely, it left just a trace of a cadence, which I should never have acquired without having first gone to the other extreme. I think this is another of those ruses to which an actor may justly resort when he is faced with a problem.

Even so I was not saved from James Agate in *The Sunday Times*:

". . . Third place is honourably won by Mr. Denys Blakelock as Johnnie, who, at 10.20 precisely, broke into the Gaelic for half-a-dozen words, and the one and only time of the evening . . ."

George, the youngest of the family, was played by Stephen Haggard, who off the stage was all I should have liked to be: cultured and knowledgeable about everything to do with the arts. Someone close to him admitted that he was intolerant of those with lesser minds than his. He certainly made me feel inferior. Stephen and I were less *en rapport* then than we could have been today.

But as I have confessed I suffered from "actor's disease" and it broke out badly. Stephen had great charm and in his part he could exercise it. George was a winning character. Johnnie, that I played, was a dour, humourless Scot who lost his girl to his brother and the love of the audience as well. This was too much!

In addition, like the Scots actors in the company, he taught me how to act; and from him I could not take it well, because he was many years my junior. Also, his friend and biographer Christopher Hassall said that, had Stephen survived the war, he would not have been an actor but a writer. I can believe this. Certainly his novel, *Nya*, was skilfully done and I believe he had written beautiful poetry too. But as an actor I thought Stephen's work never came up to his uncouth boy in *The Maitlands*, a very early appearance which, to me, was proved by after events to be more a piece of happy casting than a display of genuine virtuosity. There was always something raw about him: real and relaxed but in my opinion lacking in technical accomplishment. However, Stephen Haggard's sensitive, unusual looks and strongly individual personality could never fail to interest and attract. He is a great loss to the world of art and was mourned by many as a friend. In addition to his novel, *Nya*, he left behind one important little work for young actors: a book in the form of letters, which he wrote with Athene Seyler, called *The Craft of Comedy*.

Since that first disappointing run of *The Silver Cord* there had been many such experiences with parts and plays, which for various reasons have not appeared in the pages of this book; and now *The Black Eye*, too, had been another black season for me. The familiar mood of melancholy had set in and stage hysteria was not unknown. On the contrary it ran me into serious trouble for the first time. At the end of the play one night I could hardly speak, when I had to call Haggard out to give him the black eye of the title. It was unfortunate that it was a packed Saturday audience and that the author's wife was in the front row. It was reported to Cochran, who wrote me a letter of reprimand and reproach. In my note of apology I told him the simple truth: that there had been no frivolity, that it was a breakout of a nervous symptom. I wrote a similar letter to the producer. How dissimilar were the replies. Ayliff's letter was a schoolmaster's, cold and unyielding. Cochran, the human, warm-hearted showman, wrote by return, assuring me of his complete sympathy and understanding.

But there were happier times ahead, professionally at any rate, as that decade of the 'Thirties wore on to its disastrous end. Two plays particularly I should like to comment upon.

The first, *Indoor Fireworks*, an amusing light comedy by Arthur Macrae. This stands out in my mind chiefly on account of Fay Compton. I knew her but had never before worked with her. No one writing of the stage at the period I am covering could surely fail to make reference to this beautiful and remarkable woman of the theatre.

Fay Compton is a superb actress. There seems to be nothing in the field of dramatic art that she cannot do with equal facility and virtuosity. Her Ophelia to Barrymore's Hamlet, her exquisite performance of Barrie's *Mary Rose* cannot be forgotten; and she was the best Principal Boy I have ever seen. The sincerity of her acting, her charming singing voice, and her beautiful clear diction brought the Pantomime figure of Robin Hood at Drury Lane to life. Fay Compton is the best example I know of one who has put into effect the advice given to me by Robert Courtneidge (Cicely's father): to have a go at everything and not to attempt to put up your plate in Harley Street until you have been in general practice.

Fay Compton is an artist but there is no nonsense about her. She has a businesslike attitude towards her work, which is the hallmark of the true professional. This and her friendliness and her exceptionally quick sense of humour make her a joy to work with.

When I was with her, Fay had an old house in the country not far from Wrotham; and one Sunday I went down there for the day. There is not the slightest doubt that the house was haunted by a malevolent spirit. After tea I led our hostess on to tell us the story of the manifestations of that unhappy soul. Many very alarming things had happened in the house, which could only be explained by the presence there of some departed spirit who could not be at rest. There was one particular room upstairs where, on several occasions, the partly-opened door had been firmly held against someone trying to enter, although the room was found to be unoccupied. This creepy story took about three-quarters of an hour to tell and lost nothing in the telling from the lips of an actress like Fay Compton, with her sense of drama, her significant inflections and her passionate interest in these mysterious phenomena. It was quite dark before I left and, as I headed towards the cheerful lights of London, I could not help feeling glad that I had not arranged to stay the night. Heather Thatcher told me afterwards that she and Ivy St. Helier slept in adjoining rooms and kept the communicating door open all night long.

Laurence Olivier tried his wings as a director for the first time ever in 1935. The play was *Golden Arrow*, by Sylvia Thompson, the novelist, and Victor Cunard. Olivier asked me to be in it. This was the first time we had worked together since *St. Bernard* and the only occasion of my playing for him after he came into his own; although he offered me a part in *Daphne Laureola* which I was not in a position to accept.

Golden Arrow was a smart play and I was a smart American with a "Ritzy" accent, on which I rather plumed myself. Larry liked it too, I remember. It was based on the speech of a mutual American friend of ours, Karl Tiedemann. James Agate was not so pleased with it, he told me, when he turned up suddenly one night and took me out to supper. But he did not say so in his *Sunday Times* review. In that he wrote:

"Mr. Denys Blakelock gives the air of a cream cheese exuding venom, in that dead white voice which this delicious actor uses indifferently for Lorenzo, Aristophanes and any other gigolo."

I have a theory about accents. Actors very seldom achieve complete authenticity, unless perhaps in their own regional dialects. But if an actor has a good ear and can keep up the accent all the time without slipping out of it, and if he is himself convinced that he is reproducing the music of his model, then he will make the audience accept it. Of course there will always be those tiresome friends of yours who will be critical, just because they know your own cadences so well. James Agate acquired a bee in his bonnet about me and my accents at that time, as I have shown from his joke at my expense in *The Black Eye*.

Ernest Thesiger told me that he took infinite trouble to get an authentic accent for his perfect performance of the ghillie in *Mary Rose*. He went to the fountain-source, a native of the Hebrides. But it was such a special kind of Scottish speaking that it was dismissed by the critics as not coming from Scotland at all.

Playing opposite Olivier in *Golden Arrow* was a newcomer with little experience, but more than her share of all that goes to make a star— Greer Garson. The play was not a success, but this young actress was. She ultimately disappeared to Hollywood and is best remembered as Mrs. Miniver of the war-time film.

In *Golden Arrow* Olivier did a piece of production that was in vogue at that time. I think it was started by Tyrone Guthrie in Joyce Carey's *Sweet Aloes* at Wyndham's. The idea was to have a number of people in a room in groups talking over and through each other, in the way we do in real life. It only lasted half a minute or so and in theory it seemed a good piece of naturalism. But I always felt it confused the audience and made them feel they were missing something they ought to hear. Anyhow, it was a practice that was soon abandoned. One never sees it done now.

I wish there were something more positively interesting to record about that first Olivier production. But the play, though witty and entertaining, was very lightweight and did not give him much chance to stretch his imaginative powers. His own performance was immaculate as ever. So were his clothes. Olivier was then at his most smart and sophisticated—quite a different personality from what we know today. I think it was the phase when he had a small moustache and took pleasure in his resemblance to Ronald Colman. He had travelled far already since the days when Clare Eames had said, "Larry looks down at me with the eyes of a conqueror". The conqueror had arrived. The building of his Empire was about to begin.

CHAPTER XVIII

In 1936 the powerful name of H. M. Tennent Ltd. was seen upon the playbills for the first time. This management started off at the Queen's Theatre with a piece adapted from *The Ante-Room*, the novel by Kate O'Brien.

For me it is mainly memorable for my meeting with its author. I was already obsessed with her work: especially with her best-selling novel, *Without My Cloak*, the only book I have ever read three times. There was no disappointment in the encounter. Kate O'Brien proved to be a romantic personality. She might have materialised from the pages of one of her own stories. Her voice, with that slight, yet un-mistakable, cadence of the cultured Irish, was one of the most charming I have ever heard. It would have served her well had she decided to be an actress, instead of becoming the scholar and the incomparable writer that she is today.

Kevin Casey, playwright and poet and one of the new generation in her own country, recently said in an article that the young Irish writer of today should look for example, not to James Joyce, but to Kate O'Brien, whose book, *The Ante-Room*, was the model of what a novel should be. She told me that she herself feels that, of the many she has written, *The Ante-Room*, in form and discipline, is her best.

It was a great disappointment and a surprise to us all that as a play this moving story did not take on. It is difficult to say why this was so. Guthrie McClintic came over from America to direct it; and it was lavishly presented in the style one now associates with a Tennent production. It is true that Jessica Tandy as Marie-Rose ran away with the acting; and that had the effect of putting the play slightly out of balance. Agnes, the leading rôle, needed a tragedienne. The beautiful Diana Wynyard, who played it and who was so delightful in comedies and so resourceful a character actress in plays like Ustinov's *Photo Finish*, was not to my mind a tragedienne. She had not the deep and moving tones that tragedy demands.

I enjoyed myself exceedingly as the brother: a sad syphilitic, whiling away the empty hours of his shattered life for ever playing Chopin in his mother's drawing-room, while she lay dying upstairs.

I did not get to know Kate O'Brien really well at the time of *The Ante-Room*. It was not, in fact, until thirty years later that we caught up with each other and became close friends. She is wise, humorously philo-sophical—a stimulating and enriching companion; and the romantic aura surrounding her remains for me undiminished by the years.

There was one play in the 'Thirties which in itself was no more than clever and amusing and contributed little to theatre history. But every-one connected with the original cast was, or was to become, so cele-brated that I could hardly pass it over. I can say that, because I myself only joined *Short Story* half-way through the run, taking over from Rex Harrison who left to go to America. I fancy that it was from that time onwards that he really began to move towards his present position. An instinctive light comedian, with his flexible voice and infinite variety of notes and intonations.

The author of the play was Robert Morley, then a quite unknown actor. Later his performance of Oscar Wilde at the Gate Theatre brought him to the foreground. He was exactly the same as he is now: witty, entertaining, a great personality. The producer was Sir Tyrone Guthrie, a man I admire for his detachment from the less worthwhile things that attract so many men of the theatre. He once prophesied that I should come into my own when I was older. He was right. It was at least another ten years before I did.

Marie Tempest, not yet then Dame Marie, headed the cast. The Queen of Comedy. Who could write a book that had anything to do with the theatre of the 1900's without mentioning her? A great comedienne and a great artist. It is sad that nobody has written her biography since she died. Hector Bolitho was writing one when I was with her. It was published later, but he was handicapped by the fact that Marie Tempest was not the kind of woman who could look at herself objectively. She could never have taken the truth, especially in print. She, who had made millions laugh and would laugh delightedly at a good story, had little sense of humour about herself. She behaved like a Queen and held court at the back of the stage between her scenes. Every man, especially, was expected to play the courtier. She sat, a screen shielding her from the draught, in a comfortable upright chair, with a table and an ashtray at her side, and beneath her on the floor a drugget to protect her dress. Her husband, Willie Graham Browne, also in the cast, would keep her happy and amused during the evening. If you told him a good story he would say, "Tell that to Mary."

I had been warned beforehand that, fastidious to a degree, she par-ticularly disliked the touch of hands that were at all hot or damp; nor would she hesitate to draw attention to such things. I always took the

Ernest Milton as Hamlet

Ivor Novello

precaution of dabbing my fingers and palms with eau-de-cologne before playing the scene with her. But I noticed from the start that she never allowed you to hold her hands for more than a second or two. To avoid contact she had developed a method of her own by which she somehow contrived to take the initiative and get hold of you by the wrists.

Marie Tempest was not beautiful. She was a *jolie laide*. Although she was over seventy years of age, she seemed charged with a special quality of her own, electric and magnetic. The exhilaration I felt as she took hold of me was something like what a swimmer feels when he is lifted up and borne shorewards on the crest of a wave.

Her vitality showed itself most plainly in her eyes. Small, of a startling periwinkle-blue, and brimming with *joie de vivre*, they darted to and from your left eye and your right in a manner peculiar to her. And who could forget those tiny feet, or the small, beautiful hands, the fingers of which she used to "rouge down to the first knuckles", to add, so she told me, to the appearance of delicacy.

Everything about Marie Tempest was delicate; delicate and elegant as a French clock ticking away on some drawing-room mantelpiece; and her acting technique had the same exquisite precision as the works of a clock. If latterly, because she did not strive to recreate for every new performance, you could glimpse through the glass door the wheels going round and the pendulum swinging, that did not detract from the flawlessness of the mechanism itself.

Marie Tempest suffered from "comedianitis". That is to say she did not care for other people to steal a scene from her by getting too many laughs. The great "offender" in *Short Story* was a little-known actress called Margaret Rutherford. It was in that play that this delightful personality first made her name. I was concerned in a scene with her and Marie Tempest. We stood on either side of her. As Margaret Rutherford got laugh after laugh, Mary used to look at me and make faces and drum impatiently with those delicate fingers on the sofa arms.

She used to send messages through the stage manager: "Will Miss Rutherford kindly be quicker in the first act?" No notice was taken. Miss Rutherford had character. At last she was bidden to go to the star's dressing-room. This is a rough transcript of the dialogue that took place:

M.T. Miss Rutherford, you must be quicker in that first act scene. Hurry up, hurry up! We can't hang about all the evening. We want to get home.
(pause)

D

M.R. Miss Tempest, you've been very frank with me. I will be
equally so with you. I have a feeling in that scene that I'm being
pushed. And when I get that feeling it has the effect of making me
go slower.

(Longer pause)

Even Marie Tempest was apparently nonplussed by this rejoinder.
She respected moral courage. After that she proceeded to show
Margaret Rutherford round the photographs in her room, and
that night at the curtain call Margaret felt a friendly pat on her
shoulder.

As for Dame Margaret, as she is now, she seemed to me never to
look back after that play finished. Since then, she has shown herself to
be not only a brilliantly eccentric comedienne, but a resourceful
character actress and a beautiful reader of poetry.

The leading man in *Short Story* was A. E. Matthews: Matty as he
was called. He was then well into his seventies; still the nonchalant,
carefree man-about-town, still able to enjoy riding on the Blackpool
sands with the pretty young understudy from New Zealand, with
whom he was obviously *épris*.

Finally Sybil Thorndike. How can one write about Dame Sybil?
What can one say about her that most people do not know already?
She belongs to everyone, is a national institution.

I saw a good deal of her when we went on tour with *Short Story*.
On the day she was expecting news of the birth of her first grandchild
I took her to see Stokesay Castle in Shropshire; and at Blackpool we
stayed at the same hotel and had meals together. But she did not eat
supper in the dining-room with me. She said she preferred "a glass of
milk and a Thin Captain" in her room.

I had known Dame Sybil for many years, but until this particular
engagement I had never acted with her or had the opportunity of much
real talk with her. It is true that on one occasion she had said to me
over a table in a restaurant, "You're a 'Roman' aren't you?" (as if I
were something out of *Julius Caesar*). And when I replied in the affirma-
tive she said, "Are you ardent?"

Sybil Thorndike is herself an "ardent" Anglican. I used to feel, when
I saw them together, that Marie Tempest had a sort of grudging envy
of Sybil's goodness; that deep down she knew that her career, her
riches, her illustrious name, all the adulation she received—none of
this could compare in value with the qualities of character and the
spiritual gifts possessed by this woman whom everyone loved and

nobody feared. Certainly you could not have found two women more dissimilar. Mary spent every penny she earned on purple and fine linen and the good things of this world. Sybil, on the other hand, hates living in style; and as regards food she would not know whether she was eating peacocks' tongues or a hard-boiled egg.

There are some who would say that Marie Tempest was heartless. I do not think that entirely true. I suppose she was not what you would call a very deep character; and she had been too consistently successful, had known too little of the cares of this world and too much of the deceitfulness of riches, to be able to be greatly aware of the sorrows round about her. But she certainly loved Willy Graham Browne; and though her indomitable will forced her to lift up her head and go on acting after he died, the sense of desolation must have been acute, and Marie Tempest in those last two or three years a very lonely old woman.

I had this letter from her when I wrote to congratulate her upon being made a Dame of the British Empire:

> 55 Avenue Road,
> Regent's Park, N.W.8.
> 16 May '37

Dearest Denys,

Thank you for your sweet letter. As you say, had my darling lived to share this Honour with me it would have made all the difference. As it is, life is empty and my heart very sore.

I do hope that something will turn up for *both* of us, for it is the only means of oblivion for me—and a little money!

> My dear love to you,
> Mary

The theatre of the 'Thirties did not hold much more that was remarkable for me. But before going on to other matters there are two personalities that I would not like to leave unmentioned.

Somewhere within that decade I was concerned in the trial week in the suburbs of a new play; not the kind of piece one writes about, although it did reach Shaftesbury Avenue. I used to call for Margaret Scudamore with my car as I crossed London and convey her to the wilds of Wimbledon. Sitting in the back on one occasion was Margaret's son. He looked like a young schoolmaster, which he was. He was quiet and uncommunicative. He might have been unhappy. He *must* have been bored. Knowing now his good mind and instinctive taste for all that is best in the theatre, I can imagine what he must have thought of that farce.

But the farce was soon forgotten, and forgotten too the son of Margaret Scudamore; until many years later I went to see an Old Vic production of *The Country Wife*; and there, playing the leading part of Mr. Horner, was Michael Redgrave, tall and elegant in his Restoration wig and costume, an obvious star personality. My mind went back to those Wimbledon drives, and to the unsmiling young man with the submerged personality with whom I had been unable to make contact. With the young Redgrave, as with the young Olivier, one could never have imagined the potentialities that there lay hidden.

From the moment when at a later stage I saw him in *Winter Journey* onwards, I knew that by constant study and the tortuous routes of experimentation, Michael Redgrave had become one of the actors in our contemporary theatre who could be called great. I have missed few of his performances since that day.

His contribution to the theatre has been prodigal; and in more ways than one. Have we not to thank him and his beautiful wife, Rachel Kempson, for the gift of three talented children? Lynn and Corin I have seen so far once only each; she miraculously funny in *Hay Fever* at the National Theatre, he exactly right in *Chips With Everything*. As for Vanessa, I can only say that Eleanor Farjeon always told me she was the nearest thing to Ellen Terry we could ever hope to see. From her Rosalind alone I would guess that Vanessa Redgrave is a better actress even than Ellen was; and her great beauty and quality of poetic enchantment must surely run the famous actress's very close.

I have written nothing so far about the actor whom I think, if asked, I should put right at the top of all: that mysterious, almost uncanny near-genius, Alec Guinness. He does not act. He just disappears—like the Lawrence he portrayed so brilliantly—into the character he is concerned with. There is no personal exploitation; only that perfect interior identification that is the truth.

For many years I had not the slightest idea what he looked like off the stage. I would not have recognised him had I met him in the street. Guinness and I did not, in fact, meet until long after the war, when I went with Eleanor Farjeon to see his Hamlet at the New Theatre and visited him afterwards in the dressing-room. But since then we have met often by chance and have corresponded many times. Guinness, like myself, is a convert to Roman Catholicism. We speak the same language. He understood what I meant when I wrote congratulating him on his knighthood and said I knew he would wear it where a Franciscan wears his scapular—next his skin.

I feel I know him better than I do. He once invited me to stay with him and his wife at their house near Petersfield. But by then my curious dread of staying in strange houses had long ago crept up on me and become a fixed phobia. So I was forced to give Alec the same answer that I had given Olivier. I was greatly distressed; and felt I had missed a chance of getting to know a rare and valuable human being really well.

CHAPTER XIX

IT WAS IN the June of 1938 that we had moved into Woburn Square. During the previous years war-clouds had been rolling up thick and fast and the following September brought the Munich crisis upon us. After that had subsided we began to realise that preparations for the possibilities of warfare from the air might be seriously advisable. Slogans such as A.R.P. or R.I.P. looked menacingly at us from the hoardings.

One evening I took myself to the Fire Station in Edgware Road and offered my services as an Auxiliary Fireman. I chose this particular form of National Service because of the claustrophobia element. I felt that whatever might be demanded of a war-time fireman it would at least go on above ground.

Men who wore glasses were precluded from the A category; so I enlisted in the B class, which comprised all the duties of the full fire-fighter, except that they were not allowed to go up the ladders.

Nevertheless, there was one memorable afternoon when I looked in for instruction, which was being given by a young fireman who apparently did not know of the embargo on glasses. I was too ashamed of being thought afraid to remind him of it, and was roped in for the perilous procedure of hook-ladder drill. A few minutes later I found myself sitting astride a window-sill, which was much too far away from *terra firma* for my taste, trying with desperate unconcern to hook a ton-weight ladder on to the sill above me. It was the only occasion on which I have ever wished that I had chosen to be a window-cleaner instead of an actor. However, my guardian angel took over at this point. Just as it came to my turn to ascend the ladder to a greater height still, an older fireman took over the instruction and the moment he saw my horned-rimmed glasses he sent me down immediately.

Even in Class B I was not very successful. I had never been a Boy Scout and I am far from practical with my hands; so that all the knots we had to learn to tie presented a problem. After a time I descended further, into Class C, and threw myself once more into the training in an exaggerated, over-anxious manner; wandering about the Park, mugging up details about fire-fighting appliances and Fire Brigade personnel; tramping the streets from Lord's Cricket Ground to the regions of Maida Vale and the Harrow Road, in an endeavour to become *au fait* with the necessary routes.

One item particularly of all the things I had to learn has stuck in my mind. When you entered all the details of a fire in the duty-room book, there were certain circumstances in which you wrote: "One woman escaped *by irregular means*." This meant that the lady in question had had the impertinence to make her own way out of the burning building, instead of being carried out in the arms of a fireman.

In June or July of 1939 I passed the examination and was able to relax until such time as hostilities might break out. In that event we should be wanted at once; and we had very definite instructions as to what to do.

But for me things were to take a different turn from what I had expected. One day in early August I was struck down by a serious virus in my throat. I went to bed with a high temperature that raged for about five days; and on that hot Bank Holiday was carried off in an ambulance to the Hospital of SS. John and Elizabeth. A few days before war was declared, I was prematurely rushed out of hospital and out of London while the going was good. The actual outbreak of war found me, not as I had anticipated, sitting behind a sandbagged fire-alarm in Maida Vale, but recuperating by the sea at Woolacombe.

It is not my intention to dwell upon the war period. We went through it and had enough of it; we all had our air raid experiences and inflicted on each other anecdotes about our own private and particular bomb. I shall confine myself to the life we in the theatre contrived to live under war conditions.

My own position was that my recent illness had left me unfit for the duties of an Auxiliary Fireman; and various attempts at different branches of A.R.P. proved unsuccessful on account of the claustrophobic aspect. On these grounds, too, I found myself unconditionally rejected by the Army Medical Board. I became a voluntary fire-watcher; and for the rest I did my own job—acting and broadcasting— to the best of my ability. It was little enough; but I hope that perhaps the work we did in the theatre was of some help to those of whose courage and endurance so much more was demanded.

There was a cartoon in one of the newspapers during the war: a drawing of two cows descending side by side from a cattle-truck on to the platform. One was saying to the other: "My dear! It was disgraceful. We were herded together just like human beings."

About three weeks after the declaration of war I returned from Woolacombe in a railway carriage so packed that it gave me a foretaste of what was going to happen. The first thing I did was to buy a bicycle, which solved some of my problems in London at any rate for the rest of the war years.

It was a dismal experience at first to ride down into the West End round the familiar streets; to see those theatres which had been the scene of so much excitement and activity, so many glittering first nights, so many gay parties, all closed now; the doors locked and bolted, the vast auditoriums dark, empty, silent. Would one ever hear again that knock on the door, the young voice echoing down the stone passages, "Overture and beginners please . . ." "All down for the finale please"? It seemed then that it was *finale* indeed. One felt as if one would never act again.

But by slow degrees, one after another, the theatres began to open up. And in the early part of that first winter of the war I myself began to rehearse for a new play at the Whitehall, *Who's Taking Liberty?* by Pamela Frankau. It was good to be working again in those depressing days, and it was surprising how even I became accustomed to getting about London in the black-out. But it had its special terrors for me; and it was not long before I was burning a nightlight in my room as my father had done. It looks as if it will burn there now till it becomes a yellow taper.

In the end it was all the ramifications of the black-out and the crowded conditions of war-time travel that were to put me very nearly out of business. Just as in 1920 I had abandoned the Tube as a means of transport, so now in 1940 I had to decide to give up going even by ordinary train. As new productions invariably went on long provincial tours before coming to London, this ruled me out of the West End runs. It appeared as if a little broadcasting was the most that I could expect.

However, things were not so bad after all. In 1941 I was asked to take over a part at the Haymarket in a play which had already done the provincial tour; and there I had a nine months' run during that quiet period when the Germans had ceased their bombing. The play was *No Time For Comedy* by S. N. Behrman. Just before the war I had had a cable from Guthrie McClintic offering me a part in it. He wanted me to take over in New York and tour the States when the run finished. Katharine Cornell had played the lead over there; the rôle taken by Diana Wynyard in London. Arthur Macrae was leaving to join the R.A.F. and I was asked to replace him in the part I had been offered by McClintic and had refused. This was a particularly fortunate arrangement for me, as they had already done a long tour before opening in

London and my usual difficulty in accepting the work did not arise. So there I was back on familiar ground but playing at unfamiliar hours. We gave a matinée every day, and twice a week an evening performance at six o'clock.

In that piece at the Haymarket I was dressed by a Dame—a Pantomime Dame. He was not retired either; for sure enough when November came he left me to go into a provincial Christmas Pantomime. Mother Goose was his great rôle, and he spoke of it in much the same way that an old tragedian might refer to his Hamlet. And, as the latter could recall a beautiful Ophelia, my Dame would say of a past colleague, "'E made a luvlee Goose." Once he said, talking of Dame technique, "They used to say *when in doubt show yer drawers*; but I never would show mine." Despite this sense of propriety I learned later that his jokes were of a particularly *risqué* variety. He was very illiterate. John Gielgud's surname was quite beyond him; and of Diana Wynyard he said, "Nice unassoomin' woman, that Miss Windwood; you wouldn't know she was an actress to see 'er walk down the street."

Like all his sort he was kind-hearted, and competent and conscientious as a dresser. He lived alone at Brixton and had the sad face so often seen in those who have spent their lives in making others laugh. He died some years ago; or I would not now be writing this of him.

Many Pantomime artists fill in the periods of unemployment with dressing at a theatre. My next experience of this nature was of a Cat. "I shall be leaving you soon," he told me one evening to my surprise. "I'm going into Panto . . . Yes; I play Cat. I'm known as the finest Cat in the business," he purred in soft Scottish tones. And he was. A few years later he was starred as Dick Whittington's Cat in a big West End Pantomime. I was proud to have been dressed by him.

Soon after Christmas, in 1942, *No Time For Comedy* came to an end. I found myself in the same quandary as I was before I joined the cast; except that after a nine months' run I had been able to recoup my finances. But where was the next engagement to come from? Managements were taking advantage more and more of the thriving condition of theatre business in the Provinces by recovering their production expenses on tour before bringing plays to London. This meant that the chance of my being offered parts which I could accept was becoming increasingly remote. I sat twiddling my thumbs for a couple of months and then things began to happen.

One Sunday early in April I read in the paper that Alec Clunes had taken over the Arts Theatre and was forming a company of a semi-permanent nature and with a settled policy: to do revivals of the classics and good modern plays, and to produce new experimental works unlikely to be done by commercial managements.

On the Monday morning I had a call from Alec Clunes and went along to see him, walking down as usual from my flat in Bloomsbury. As I approached that junction in Upper St. Martin's Lane where seven roads meet how little I thought of all that was waiting for me round that next corner.

Alec Clunes was businesslike but beguiling.

"We are going to do *Twelfth Night*," he said. "Will you come and play Aguecheek for us?"

"Oh no, Alec, I couldn't," I replied, running away as usual. I was remembering Lorenzo and what James Agate had said about me as a Shakespearean actor.

Then he went on to tell me that they were opening with *Awake and Sing* by Clifford Odets, and he gave me the choice of two parts. I refused both—and Aguecheek. But Clunes persuaded me to go home and think the matter over.

I left the Arts Theatre in a whirl of indecision, and there is little doubt that my answer that evening would have been in the negative—but for one unforeseen factor. Later in the morning I had to go to see the psychiatrist with whom I was having some treatment. He was merciless. He accused me of having run away from everything all my life; and said that if I continued to play for safety in this manner I should get nowhere. It had a profound effect on me and I went home a much-chastened man. That psychiatric session was to have a far-reaching effect on me professionally. From this time onward I so-to-speak substituted a policy of attempt for a policy of avoidance; and in the years that followed found myself doing things in the theatre which, up to that time, I would have thought to be right outside the range to which I had limited myself. I began, that very afternoon, as I read and re-read the text of *Twelfth Night*, to see what I had been missing all these years. I saw that Sir Andrew Aguecheek was a very real human being, lovable and touching. Of course I could play him. I *would* play him.

But first there was the hurdle of Sam Feinscriber in *Awake and Sing*. Sam as a character could have hardly been further away from my own personality, but it was a part for which I felt immediate sympathy and understanding. His origin is never stated, but I always thought of him as Polish-American.

So that afternoon in my flat, having come to terms with *Twelfth*

Night, I browsed over this disturbing play of Jewish family life in the Bronx. I went into a self-induced, semi-hypnotic trance over Sam; and suddenly from somewhere—from nowhere—a voice came. An accent and something more than an accent, because the quality of the sound was quite different, unrecognisable as my own. I began to get that mysterious sense of identification which I have always experienced when I have done my best work. I knew I had found Sam Feinscriber. He and Sir Andrew were embryonically alive within me. Feeling strangely excited, I picked up the telephone and dialled Temple Bar 7541. This time it was a firm "Yes" to Alec Clunes.

Awake and Sing opened in May 1942 and gave a flying start to the Arts Theatre Group of Actors. Richard Attenborough, fresh from the R.A.D.A., was eighteen and would, I am sure, be the first to agree that his part was an exceptional opportunity for the start of a young actor's career. In all the publicity that has been put out about him since then I have never heard or seen *Awake and Sing* mentioned. The part he played later in *The Little Foxes* at the Piccadilly is always recorded as his first London appearance. I am sure Attenborough himself is not to blame for this. It is simply the way of the publicity-hound with his material.

My Sam in *Awake and Sing* was an unexpected success. So was Sir Andrew with which I followed it. In the case of Aguecheek I was told that Ernest Milton had described Sir Andrew as a case of arrested development. This gave me something to start from and I approached him from that point of view. Alec Clunes, who produced the play, made capital from my diffidence. Instead of doing anything exaggerated in the part, I *under*did everything. Even with "Faith I can cut a caper" I did no Illyrian fling; but with a great show raised my foot a few inches from the ground only to lose confidence and put it down again.

Not only did I play Sam and Sir Andrew, but I remained at the Arts on and off for nearly three years; taking no less than twelve parts, all of a widely contrasted nature, including three completely different characters in a burlesque of *Maria Marten*, from one to the other of which, as an old-time, protean actor, I had to do lightning changes throughout the evening.

All this greatly added to my confidence; I found myself doing things which a few months before I should never in my most optimistic moments have contemplated. It was as if for all those years I had been paddling about in the shallow end of the swimming bath; and now was being induced not only to dip a tentative toe in the deep end, but to

take a running dive off the highest board. My new policy was working
well. But I must say here that these successes in a new field and others
that were to follow I owed as much to Alec Clunes as I did to my new-
found policy of attempt. He led me on gently but firmly towards parts
for which no other management had ever thought of me, and which,
had they done so, I should have been afraid to undertake.

It seemed ironical that I, who had been on the London Stage for
twenty years, should now find myself doing the kind of hard work
from which I had run away as a young man. I learned during this
period for the first time the joy of doing good work for the work's
sake; with no possibility, as I thought then, of material advantage. We
received, in that first year or so at the Arts, a salary of five pounds a
week, though it increased a little later on. But when, at the end of the
war, I returned to the commercial theatre, the work I had done in those
lean years had so improved my professional standing that I found my
pre-war salary doubled and my name in a star position on the bills. It
would seem that virtue—even when forced upon one by circumstances
—does bring its own reward. Certain it is, in my experience, that most
of the things one runs away from in life one is made to face up to later
on.

In the summer of 1943 Alec Clunes put on an Arts Theatre Festival.
The three plays in which I was involved were *The Rivals*, Pinero's *The
Magistrate*, and *The Watched Pot* by "Saki".

In *The Rivals* I played the famous rôle of Bob Acres and I think I
was good, in a different way from the usual representation. I feel very
strongly about Acres that to play him as a bucolic is quite wrong. Had
he been an uncouth countryman of that kind he would never have been
the familiar friend of Mrs. Malaprop and Lydia Languish, who were
distinctly "upper class". I think "fighting Bob" is a sort of second
cousin to Sir Andrew Aguecheek; a little simple and immature, un-
versed in the ways of fashionable London life, because he has always
lived in the depths of the country. Hence his name, Acres.

Perhaps all this is only an alibi for the fact that I could not have
played him any other way; but I am supported by Joseph Jefferson
who made the part his own throughout America. He discusses the
character at some length in his autobiography. His granddaughter,
Eleanor Farjeon, told me he played it on light comedy lines, as opposed
to the traditional low comedy approach. Irving, Ellen Terry and John
Hare, all of whom saw Jefferson's Acres in America, were entranced
with his performance. So much so that Hare expressed the wish that it
could be seen in the London theatre. Jefferson, however, decided

against it as he felt it would not be acceptable here. Apart from his rendering of Acres, he had taken various liberties with the play itself and had condensed the original five acts into three. Even in his own country this had been criticised by the traditionalists. But Jefferson says in his autobiography that he felt justified in doing what he did with *The Rivals* in view of Sheridan's adaptation of *The Relapse* into *A Trip To Scarborough*.

The Rivals and *The Magistrate* opened within a night or two of each other and we rehearsed them concurrently. This was an exhausting and alarming experience for me, who had picked my professional path so carefully for years, and had always avoided doing more than one thing at a time if possible. But if it was exhausting it was exciting too; and that Festival period was, I think, the most fruitful and creative phase in my life as an actor.

CHAPTER XX

THE MAGISTRATE IS a good subject with which to start a new chapter of this book, because it was that play that began a new chapter in my career. Knowing how tedious we actors can be about our past successes, I shall try to write of this one as objectively as possible, though without that false modesty which is as unattractive as its ugly sister, self-praise.

When Alec Clunes told me that Mr. Posket, the name part in *The Magistrate*, was one of the three he had earmarked for me in the Festival, I panicked. My old habit of avoidance reasserted itself. It seemed far too large a part for me to undertake; and I could see no way in which I would characterise it. I had always found it difficult to "put on" age; and Posket, though not an old man according to modern reckoning, is a Victorian magistrate and demands a certain weight and authority. I baulked at *The Magistrate* and once more found myself saying "No" to Alec Clunes. He returned to the attack and in despair I had another private session with Mr. Posket. Once again I induced the trance-like mood; and, as with Aguecheek and Sam, something began to happen. I agreed to try to play the part after all.

When rehearsals began I worked as I have always worked since my earliest student days. That is to say, apart from the rehearsals with the producer and company I did a tremendous amount of homework. This meant for me setting the scene, with furniture and props, as far as was possible in my own room; and going over and over the part, until words and feeling and business and moves co-ordinated in an exactly-timed whole. The ultimate art of the actor lies, having done all this, in covering it up so that to them that see the finished performance these mechanics are indiscernible.

In most theatrical quarters, I am sure, my way of going to work would be considered finicky and unnecessary. But I discovered recently that at least one other colleague studies in the same way: that brilliant artist Patience Collier. However, there are as many "methods" of acting as there are actors. This was mine; and in support of my meticulousness in the matter of mechanics, I will quote George Henry Lewes in *On Actors and the Art of Acting*. He is writing of Edmund Kean:

"One who often acted with him informed me that, when Kean was rehearsing on a new stage, he accurately counted the number of steps he had to take before reaching a certain spot, or before uttering a certain word."

Before I leave this point I will quote from a recent letter I had from Alec Clunes on the subject of our work together:

"One of my best remembered joys was waiting each morning to see what you had cooked up (or refined) during your painstaking hours of homework."

The Magistrate is so well known and has been such a standby with professional and amateur companies, that a few details about its origin and history may be of interest.

The Magistrate was produced at the Royal Court Theatre on 21st March, 1885. It was the first of the trio of famous Pinero farces (*The Schoolmistress* and *Dandy Dick* being the other two) and has remained the favourite ever since. The part of Mr. Posket has become associated in theatre history with the name of the comedian Edward Terry, who played it up and down the country for years, although the rôle was not created by him but by Arthur Cecil who was in management at the Court Theatre.

There was a great deal of discussion as to whether or not I should wear Dundreary whiskers. It was thought that, though they were amusing and would certainly add something to the personality of Mr. Posket, they belonged to a period rather earlier than the one at which we were aiming. But William, the wig-maker at Gustave's, set my mind at rest on that subject. He assured me that he remembered, as a boy, coming to work in the morning and seeing Sir Edward Clarke walking up the Strand, with his Dundrearies blowing in the wind. This was in the early 1900's; so though Sir Edward was, no doubt, behind his times, why should not Mr. Posket be behind the period in which we dressed *The Magistrate*? I felt I had ample justification for my Dundrearies.

As a consequence of the first-night notices I had a letter from Henry Ainley, written in his courteous and old-world style, from his retirement in West Acton.

> 61, Princes Gardens,
> West Acton, W.3.
> 5 August, 1943

My dear Denys Blakelock,

Good reading for you in today's Press. My hearty congratulations. The Author will be proud and happy. I wish we had the privilege of his wise counsel. He was a remarkable friend to the actor, and you have done him full square justice.

What a happy far away world it seems. And yet I was born the year before *The Magistrate* appeared in public. He and Bancroft will be reading about you in the Heavenly Court Circular, giving you their blessing. We shall not look upon their like again.

Thank you for giving them, your public and the critics such a perfect performance.

Yours happily,
Henry Ainley

After the play had opened several people mentioned Mr. Posket's walk and the stoop that was part of it. This raises an interesting point, and stresses the importance of approaching a part interiorly; that is of acting *from the inside outwards*. Provided you have plenty of rehearsing time for the character to grow within you, this interior identification, involving as it must the unconscious processes as well as the conscious, automatically creates the mannerisms of the character. If your thought is right, your walk will be right. Interior truth will produce exterior verisimilitude.

Until my attention was drawn to the stooping walk of Mr. Posket, I had not myself been aware of it. The character by that time had so taken charge that he spoke and moved and gesticulated in and through me, of his own volition.

So acting is possession. Fortunately for us, only temporary possession.

On account of my marked association with *The Magistrate* I came to be offered one character after another of the same *genre*. Judges, professors, doctors; prim, pompous and with a distinct Victorian flavour. Archbishops, Bishops, Deans, Archdeacons, every level of the Anglican hierarchy, came my way, including the last part I played in the commercial theatre, an absent-minded Vicar. They all sprang from the loins of Aeneas Posket.

I have always striven to re-create afresh for each new character, but it is only too easy to get out the printing frame and take just another copy from the Pinero negative.

From a purely business angle, an actor can console himself with the thought that it is a good thing to stand for something positive in the casting mind; but from the artistic standpoint one would like to be considered capable of doing other things. I myself have become labelled as a comedian; yet I know that I am no less able now to play parts of a serious and emotional nature than I was in the days of *The Silver Cord*.

But while I was still within the orbit of Alec Clunes he continued to give me the opportunity of ringing the changes on the characters I played. For instance in 1944 he asked me if I would like to tackle Charles Battle the stockbroker-father in Somerset Maugham's *The Bread Winner*. This had originally been created by that delightful comedian Ronald Squire. It did not sound like me; but I was becoming more and more adventurous and I took it on. It was a success; although you might not have thought so from James Agate's provocative caption over his article in *The Sunday Times*.

MR. BLAKELOCK RUINS A PLAY

I knew too well by then his puckish ways and kindly intentions; so that it never occurred to me to take this headline as anything other than one of Jimmie Agate's ambiguous, backhanded compliments. Not so my friends. Within a few hours I was receiving sympathy and commiseration on all sides. Without my knowledge a loyal friend wrote to Agate in gentle remonstrance, pointing out that such a caption could do an actor harm with managers, because they might happen to see the headline without having time to read the article underneath.

The logic of this is unanswerable; and Agate was obviously a little disturbed, lest he had perhaps gone too far and I myself might have misinterpreted his good intentions. So he replied with a letter in his own writing, sent it to me to read on the way and asked me to post it on.

> Queen Alexandra Mansions,
> Grape Street, W.C.2
> November 1, '44.

My dear Sir,
  Don't be an ass!!!
  Obviously the title "Mr. B. Ruins a Play" is *libellous* and therefore the reader who can read knows that the article beneath it must be ecstatic.
  Any actor should give both his ears for such a heading, and I am astonished that D.B. hasn't sent me at least one. . . .
> Yours sincerely,
> James Agate

Soon after this we did a season of *The Magistrate* at the St. Martin's Theatre. James Agate had been present on the first night, but when his paper came out the following Sunday there was no mention of the piece. He told me later that he had intended giving me his caption on that Sunday: *Denys Blakelock Makes a Play*, to offset the previous one. But on that one particular occasion he was asked to be the guest of *The Sunday Times* film critic, Dilys Powell, and had to devote his column to a special article on Laurence Olivier's film of *Henry V*.

CHAPTER XXI

THE ARTS THEATRE phase for me, though prolonged, was not entirely uninterrupted. There were several productions spread over those three years in which for one reason or another I did not appear. It gave me the chance to have a rest, to live a more sociable life and to see other plays. By this time my new attitude to the theatre was becoming habitual and I found myself interested in its history and anxious to miss no contemporary performance that was considered outstanding.

It was during one of my free periods that I read of Donald Wolfit's great success as King Lear, at the Scala Theatre. I had never seen the play; nor had I seen Wolfit act, except once I think in a minor part, many years before. This proved to be one of those theatre evenings all too infrequent; an evening of discovery and illumination; the discovery of a "new" actor of the classics, whose name would take a permanent place in theatre history, and the illumination of a Shakespeare character and text with which till then I had been unfamiliar. I can hear those four words now, spoken in Wolfit's splendid tones, which came to life for me as if I heard them that night for the first time: "Every inch a King."

I admired, too, the way he took his curtain calls at the end of the play. They were a work of art in themselves; and I warmed to them as a piece of legitimate showmanship, part of the true glamour of the playhouse which we are in danger of losing. I went home feeling I had had a real evening in the sort of theatre I had given my heart to in my very early days.

The next morning I wrote to Donald Wolfit. I wondered if he would even remember our last meeting twenty years previously. I had gone to Hunstanton for a holiday between engagements, and the Actors' Church Union chaplain, a saintly man called Father Kingsbury, had asked me to call on a young actor who was convalescing there. In typical seaside digs, with Bible texts as the only decoration on the walls, I found the young Donald. We met two or three times and went for walks together by the sea. He mentions these meetings in his own autobiography. He and I took very different paths: he the way of industry and application, I the easy way which I have described. No one more richly deserves his Honours than Sir Donald Wolfit, not only for his gifts and work as an actor, but for his untiring labours for the good of the theatre in war-time and in peace.

This is the letter he wrote to me in reply to mine about his performance of King Lear:

> Scala Theatre,
> Charlotte Street,
> W.1.
> 30.4.44.

Dear Denys,

Thank you for your delightful note. I am glad "Lear" satisfied you so well. It is a great struggle to do it even moderate justice.

I have *often* spoken of your kindness to me at 'Hunston' so many years ago. It was you who came and looked me up in my dreary little combined room, which I had just scraped enough to take for three weeks on doctor's orders. I only just met the bill!

I think we have met once since then only. Curious that two people occupied with the same job in the heart of London should not meet; but of course I am away half the year on tour and the cares of management give me a fourteen hour day more often than not.

I hear you are all doing grand work at the Arts, but I haven't been in alas! I wanted Clunes to play Iago with me but he couldn't. Am now desperately looking for actors of some kidney to play with me this autumn but *where* does one look and they are all Croesus. (Or should it be Croesi?!) They should try management.

All good wishes to you,

> Yours very sincerely,
> Donald Wolfit

Today I often run into Wolfit—in a club or at a theatre; or striding across the blasted heath (Hampstead) to keep himself acting fit. One can feel nothing but affection for a man so genial and friendly, so full of enthusiasm for life and work.

But to return to the Arts Theatre: I was going from strength to strength. I achieved another of my secret ambitions. I became a director. This experience was one of the few things in my life that was not even a little disappointing when I came to it. I had far more solid satisfaction and self-expression from producing other actors than I ever found in acting myself.

Alec Clunes entrusted me with two productions: *Don Abel Wrote a Tragedy*, by the Quintero brothers, and Sheridan's *A Trip to Scarborough*. In writing of the latter in *Time and Tide*, Herbert Farjeon suggested that I might be "the man many dramatic classics are looking for", which from a critic of his tastes came as a pleasing surprise.

If the classics are still looking for me, it is my own fault. In 1947 H. M. Tennent paid me the compliment of asking me to produce *The Relapse* (afterwards done so expertly by Anthony Quayle). The preliminary preparations were actually begun when I felt, in this case I think rightly, that I had bitten off more than I could chew. I had not the varied technical knowledge of stagecraft, costumes and lighting without which one is not qualified to shoulder such an undertaking. Of my own volition I withdrew. Once again I was paying for the past. This was the opportunity to which I referred in an early Chapter, which fell into my lap like a ripe apple and had to be thrown away untasted.

But at the Arts I had Alec Clunes's experience behind me; he could deal with any doubtful point at a moment's notice, leaving me free to concentrate on the play itself and on directing the actors, which I felt I did well. I was admirably served by the members of both the casts. John Ruddock was a wonderfully real and touching Don Abel; and in the Sheridan play Frith Banbury gave a highly amusing and accomplished performance of Lord Foppington. I remember Frith as almost the only actor I know to whom one could speak the absolute truth without beating about the bush, which made directing him doubly pleasurable.

Some years later, after the war, positions were reversed. Frith Banbury, by then manager and producer, directed me, when I took over from Ernest Thesiger in *Always Afternoon* by Dido Milroy at the Garrick Theatre. I hope he found me as easy to deal with—easier at any rate than the obstreperous pet rabbit which I had to nurse throughout the play and which, in amorous mood, would chew my clothes to pieces.

By 1944 I had had at the Arts Theatre the sort of experience I should have undergone as a young actor. I had made up for the deficiency, had played several big leading parts and mainly through *The Magistrate* had consolidated my position as an actor who was in demand in a wider field.

At the end of the war, in 1945, that demand began to declare itself.

CHAPTER XXII

"Why this actor is allowed to languish in highbrow holes and intellectual corners, is one of the things I have given up trying to understand."

THIS WAS JAMES AGATE'S review that appeared underneath the caption about *The Bread Winner*. Rather hard on the Arts; standing as it does in the heart of London's theatreland it could hardly be called a hole or a corner.

John Gielgud, however, supplied the answer to Agate's protest, and was the means of my returning to the commercial theatre. He was to produce *Lady Windermere's Fan* for H. M. Tennent and I was asked to play Mr. Cecil Graham.

I was delighted at the prospect of being directed for the first time by Gielgud and of playing such a well-known part in a distinguished classic. May Whitty told me that her husband, Ben Webster, was the Cecil Graham in the original production and at Oscar Wilde's behest wore the green carnation for the first time. And I learned from Lilian Braithwaite that in Sir George Alexander's two revivals of this piece, in which she herself was Lady Windermere, Cecil Graham was played in one revival by Leslie Faber and in the other by Owen Nares.

So I had something to live up to. But even I could not deny that Cecil Graham was the kind of character I knew how to deal with. In fact, I was already familiar with it; as I had played it for Val Gielgud when he did a stylish production of *Lady Windermere* on the radio a few years before the war.

John Gielgud's rehearsals were no disappointment. His inexhaustible supply of nervous energy never ceased to surprise me. When we were working on *Lady Windermere* I would as usual snatch every spare moment to relax. Not so Sir John, who would direct the complicated ballroom scene, using his full voice and standing at the back of the pit, regardless of the fact that that night he had to play Hamlet, or Ferdinand in *The Duchess of Malfi*. But then John has one invaluable gift: that of being able to forget everything and curl up like a cat at any moment, anywhere, and go fast asleep for a couple of hours.

With Gielgud as a producer one needs all one's flexibility, for he is not content with anything for long. With febrile mind and unresting imagination he constantly experiments, changing positions and invent-ing new "business" from moment to moment. Even at the Dress Rehearsal, on the morning of the opening night at Oxford, there were innovations. One of them, the figures of the dancers in the ball-room reflected on the glass of the double doors, was a last moment touch that was frequently mentioned afterwards by people in the audience.

Having opened at Oxford we were in the Provinces for two months before we came to the Haymarket. It may well seem strange that I was suddenly able at this point to do a long prior-to-London tour. The facts were these: the Tennent management knew of my inability to make the train journeys; but John Gielgud was willing for an understudy to do the tour if I could play the opening week at Oxford and join them again for the London first night. This was ideal for me; and at that time, although the petrol laws were strict, it was possible on medical grounds to obtain the permit for me to do the one week in a hired self-drive car.

However, we had not been rehearsing long before Hugh Beaumont of Tennents decided that it was important for me to remain with the company the whole time. The theatre's contribution to the war-effort in the upkeep of morale had earned it a reasonable degree of considera-tion in such matters; so the management were granted a special petrol allowance for me to fulfil my obligations, provided that the driving was limited strictly to each week-end journey from town to town. The car itself was lent me by Tennents.

So off I started that first Sunday, with John Gielgud, Mabel Terry-Lewis and Hugh Beaumont as my passengers. Although I had not driven since before the war we arrived safely in time for lunch and the first Dress Rehearsal.

That week at Oxford was a very pleasant one. In the day-time, the golden beauty of the University City in the summer term; and in the evening, the interest and excitement attached to a new, lavish Tennent production on its way to London after the unending austerities of war. From the beginning the greatest success of all was made by Cecil Beaton, whose dresses and décor were as responsible as anything for the long run of *Lady Windermere's Fan*. It was my first encounter with this gifted artist and was an experience in itself. No one would suspect, on being introduced to him, that behind that calm, collected exterior were reserves of dynamic energy; a brain and a constitution capable of an output as prodigious as it is diverse. It was fascinating to watch him at work; superintending every detail personally, putting a dress to rights, or touching up a piece of scenery here and there with his own deft brush.

I was able to clear up a point of interest to theatre historians as to the leading lady who appeared in the original production at the St. James's Theatre in 1892, when Sir George Alexander was Lord Windermere and Marion Terry played Mrs. Erlynne. The cast list in the printed copy of the play gives the name of Lily Hanbury as the first Lady Windermere. But Eleanor Farjeon, who was taken to see the piece as a child of eleven, told me that she was quite certain she had seen Winifred Emery (the late Mrs. Cyril Maude) in the part. To settle the question I got into touch with Cyril Maude himself and learned that we were both right. He wrote to say that Lady Windermere had primarily been played by "dear lovely Lily Hanbury", but through illness Winifred Emery had soon taken over. She made a great hit in the part, and presumably played it to the end. So that any theatregoers who saw the first production of *Lady Windermere* were more likely to have seen Winifred Emery than Lily Hanbury.

I was given one other authentic glimpse back into the past by Mabel Terry-Lewis, who played the Duchess of Berwick on the prior-to-London tour. This time it was of the play's author, Wilde himself.

Mabel was the daughter of Kate Terry, who left the stage while yet young to marry a rich man. They lived in a large mansion on Campden Hill: Moray Lodge. Mabel told me she remembered, as a girl, Oscar Wilde appearing at one of their parties dressed in a black velvet suit, with a yellow silk bow tie and an arum lily in his buttonhole.

CHAPTER XXIII

Now we are back in London. It is Tuesday, 21st August—the evening of our opening night at the Theatre Royal, Haymarket.

John Gielgud has given his final instructions . . . Cecil Beaton has been round with his paint brush for the last time . . . flowers, telegrams and first night presents have been arriving at the stage-door in Suffolk Street all day long . . . "Beginners" has been called . . . Leslie Bridgewater's musicians are playing the Overture . . . The lights are going down . . . the great curtain is rising . . . the first performance of the biggest success of the post-war theatre boom has begun.

It is not long before Lady Windermere's ball is in progress. Mr. Cecil Graham comes face to face with Mrs. Erlynne. "Oh, how do you do, Mr. Graham? Isn't that your aunt, Lady Jedburgh? I should so much like to know her" . . . A moment's hesitation and embarrassment . . . and Mr. Graham says: "Oh, certainly, if you wish it . . . Aunt Caroline, allow me to introduce Mrs. Erlynne . . ." The introduction of the demimondaine to the most respectable lady in London is effected—Mrs. Erlynne has won the day . . . Mr. Cecil Graham, with an amused smile on his lips, passes into the ballroom with Lady Jedburgh on his arm to join the other guests, the shadow of whose waltzing figures is to be seen upon the double doors . . .

I had a whole last act wait before I was wanted down on the stage again for the final curtain; and I was to be seen most evenings wending my way along the corridor to Athene Seyler's room. Athene, as the Duchess, had an even longer wait than mine; for after her appearances in the first two acts Oscar Wilde had given her nothing more to do. As she is a woman of many obligations and prolific activities, the time was not wasted. You would find her, perhaps, ankle-deep in correspondence at her desk, interviewing callers on one subject or another, reading a radio-script or a new play, or telephoning home instructions about the toad-in-the-hole for that night's supper.

She and I had many mutual interests, including and especially theology, and those waits of ours were taken up with friendly controversy. More than once, to prove a point, I sent the Bible to her room by the call-boy with a passage underlined.

Those half-hours in Athene Seyler's dressing-room used to pass like a flash. All too soon we would hear that voice calling as it came up the

stairs and along the passage . . . "All down for the finale, please . . ."
Outside our door now . . . "All down for the finale, please . . ." going
away, on and up to the next floor to call Mr. Beaton's Young Ladies, in
another room that I used to visit sometimes, whose interior looked
like a picture by Degas or Laura Knight. The bright scarlet dress; the
emerald green; a drooping lady of the 'nineties in ivory satin; and, in
the corner, my Aunt Jedburgh, weighed down with pearls and pen-
dants, with coronet and earrings—all sitting among the paints and pots
and powder-bowls and the usual paraphernalia of a theatrical dressing-
room.

"All down for the finale, please" . . . They are coming down the
stairs now and Athene and I are joining them . . . laughing, talking,
tripping, apologising. . . . Now we are waiting behind the scenes, while
Lord and Lady Windermere make it up and decide to live happily ever
after. . . . Now we are all streaming on to the stage, taking up our
places for the elaborately arranged calls. . . . Athene and I are together,
the theological argument is going on under our breaths. . . . The curtain is up and we are making our acknowledgments. . . . Now it is our
turn, Athene's and mine . . . we go forward, trying to collect ourselves
and smile . . . I hear Athene mutter something about the second Epistle
to the Corinthians, as we bow and turn away. . . . The applause goes
on . . . Isabel Jeans, as Mrs. Erlynne, in that unforgettable pink dress,
steps forward and makes her charming speech . . . and the curtain
comes down for the last time.

CHAPTER XXIV

IT WAS FOR the last time, so I thought, when the curtain fell at the final performance in January, 1947; for at the conclusion of *Lady Windermere* I decided to leave the stage. Despite the successful and rewarding work I had done at the Arts and at the Haymarket, I found too many things in an actor's life that warred against too many things in me.

It must appear a strange moment to have chosen; but behind the scenes there was plenty to account for it. I have made it clear that I hated long runs; this had been a very long one indeed. When our second summer came and it was known that we were to have no holidays I felt so darkly claustrophobic that without any warning I took one—on a medical certificate. This was a bold step for an actor to take; especially for an un-bold actor like me. But then if the impulses driving me are strong enough I realise now I can be very bold indeed.

And there had been another disruptive factor at work. The night after we opened I heard that my greatest friend had been sent home from active service in West Africa on a hospital ship—a mental case. From then on for me it was farewell the tranquil mind for many, many months.

After the weeks of waiting there was the first visit to the mental hospital—a new and unforgettable experience. I walked on to the stage that night at the Haymarket in a daze. Week after week I had to force myself into that sad institution; where every door you passed through locked itself behind you and you knew you could only get out by finding an orderly to unlock it. This weekly strain inevitably brought about an aggravation of the old troubles; and for most of that long time at the Haymarket I was staving off depressions and keeping anxieties at bay.

It only needed the Fuel crisis of that January, 1947, to finish me off. With my exaggerated dread of darkness and my over-fertile imagination, I envisaged a total failure of light and power throughout the country. I was in no state of mind to make decisions; but that is generally when I seem to make them. I made this one then: to finish with the theatre. At the time I thought the step a final one, but I was to see before long that the theatre had not quite finished with me yet.

One of the occupations in which I intended to interest myself was teaching; and Sir Kenneth Barnes invited me to join the staff at the R.A.D.A.

That year of 1947, when I tried to live a life away from the world where I had earned my living since I was nineteen, was not a successful one. I soon learned that it was one thing to have experimental knowledge of an art, but that to communicate it to others was an art in itself. I found the then existing conditions at the R.A.D.A. frustrating. I had a great affection for Kenneth Barnes and admired his fundamental goodness, his unwearying capacity for work, his kindness to the students and the example he set of courage in the face of many adversities in his personal life. Nevertheless, he was round about seventy and unable to get the measure of the new post-war world of the theatre. His prime concern was money for the Academy; and in order to meet its financial obligations he had to make it far too easy for stage-struck people with only a modicum of talent to gain admission. This meant that the teachers had to deal with unwieldy classes, and were compelled to neglect the talented students in order to drag along the uninspired.

I did one production, a re-production of my Arts Theatre *A Trip to Scarborough*. But the effort required of giving everyone in the huge class a fair chance by rehearsing two casts concurrently I found exhausting. After that I gave up being a producer and took the much smaller classes of men only in Diction. These were the foundation of the Audition Technique classes I was to give much later. They were one of John Fernald's innovations when he succeeded Sir Kenneth, and they proved of great practical use to the students.

Meanwhile, during that year I was getting offers to go back to the stage. I had a very understanding letter from Noël Coward, when I had to refuse a part in his play, *Peace in our Time*.

> 1, Burton Mews,
> South Eaton Place,
> London, S.W.1.
> 13.6.47.

My dear Denys,

Of course I understand absolutely perfectly. Having had nerve trouble myself in the past I sympathise with your point of view completely. Try your best to relax and emerge from the tunnel. It would be a pity were you to give up the Theatre forever as you are a fine actor,

> Yours,
> Noël

I have already mentioned my being asked by Tennents to do the Vanbrugh play from which *A Trip to Scarborough* was derived, *The Relapse*; and of my realising that my misspent theatrical life had rendered me unfit to take on such a responsible burden. This offer came during 1947. I rashly accepted it, but after four days I withdrew from the situation and gave the production over into the hands of Anthony Quayle.

I shall never forget that short period when I knew what it was to be a West End producer. Cyril Ritchard and Madge Elliot were the stars and I loved them dearly. But they were either in constant communication with me on the telephone or holding conferences in my small flat. There were casting meetings at the Globe, and costume designers and décor artists coming at me from all directions. Letters poured in from actors and actresses I had worked with and who had seen an early announcement of my production in the Press. The straw that broke the camel's back was a telephone call before I was out of bed one morning from an actor quite unknown to me asking for a job. I found myself, in fact, in a position of responsibility and authority for which I was not equipped and from which anyway I have all my life retreated.

One pleasant contact came out of those few days of being a power in the theatre world. A new young actor from Stratford, playing his first important part in London at His Majesty's, was introduced to me in the Tennent office one day. It was Paul Scofield who had been engaged for the cast of *The Relapse*. I saw him a few nights later in Peter Brook's production of *Romeo and Juliet*. I wrote to him to congratulate him on his Mercutio (the Queen Mab speech was remarkable) and to say how sorry I was not to be producing him after all. I must have written of seeing Tree play the same part and at the same theatre; and of being told of Tree's inability to learn his lines, and having them written on boards which were held up in the orchestra pit for him to see. To that letter of mine I had the following reply:

> 249, Avondale Avenue
> Esher,
> Surrey,
> 19th October 1947

Dear Mr. Blakelock,

Your letter is about the nicest one I've ever had. Thank you for it. I am more disappointed than I can say that I am not to work for you in *The Relapse*, but I look forward enormously to meeting you again.

Your word in my ear about films is very welcome, though I'm sorry you denied me your further words of wisdom!

I think it delicious that Tree didn't know his lines. It makes me feel quite smug. This letter I know is an inadequate reply to your own but it does give me the opportunity to express my appreciation of the kind things you have said—and also to tell you how sorry I am that you are not well, and that I hope you will be better very soon.

With every good wish,
Yours very sincerely,
Paul Scofield

I wonder what the "further words of wisdom" were that I denied Paul Scofield? Anyhow, their being withheld has not prevented him from having a brilliant career. In less than ten years from that time he had been awarded the C.B.E. for his work in the theatre. The rather over-used words "interesting" and "exciting" seem to have a special application in Scofield's case, with his strange handsome face, and the compelling tones of his very idiosyncratic voice. There is nothing usual or expected about him. There was always a relaxedness, a quality of abandonment, even in his early work, which was what gave to his Queen Mab speech the excitement so often missing when I have heard it done by others.* Scofield's performance in *The Family Reunion*, his priest in *The Power and the Glory*, the murderer in *A Dead Secret* and his *King Lear* I shall remember especially; and perhaps most of all the quiet dignity, the humour and the emanation of true spirituality of his St. Thomas More in *A Man for all Seasons*.

Although it was not meant that we should meet over the production of *The Relapse*, Paul and I met sooner than we expected in a radio programme. During those rehearsals we used to have tea together in a café in Great Portland Street; and I came to know his mind about many things and to feel real affection for him, as everyone still does who works with him now that he is in an authoritative position.

While we had been at the Haymarket, H. M. Tennent had tried an experiment. They had engaged the comedian Sydney Howard to play the Dean of St. Marvells, in Pinero's *Dandy Dick*, and had sent the play out on a prior-to-London tour, with A. E. Matthews in the part of Sir Tristram Mardon. Despite this cast, a clever production by

* There has since been a Mercutio so memorable that I feel it only fair to mention it. Alec McCowen, in his own quite different way, brilliantly equalled Scofield's performance of this rôle.

Irene Hentschel, and décor and costumes by Cecil Beaton, there seemed to be something wrong somewhere. Eventually we heard that *Dandy Dick* had failed to draw in the provinces and would not be coming to London. This apparently was mainly due to the fact that Sydney Howard did not easily suggest Victorian respectability; or that to shelter a race horse for the night in the Deanery stables and to back it to win in the St. Marvell's races, could be for him a matter for self-recrimination and remorse.

By 1948 I had apparently not quite got the theatre out of my blood. Nor on the other hand had I learned then to find much joy in teaching. In exactly a year of my leaving the stage Tennents asked me to return and see what I could do with the part of the Dean. This time I did not say "No" and I was soon rehearsing once again under the direction of Athene Seyler for a try-out six weeks season at the Lyric, Hammersmith.

We had only been rehearsing for a few days when history repeated itself. I had a failure of nerve and felt I could not go on. Perhaps I should explain that one aspect of this flight mechanism was that I always had a disproportionate sense of obligation towards the management and my fellow actors. My one terror was that I should let them down; therefore I tended to give up and run away much too soon. In point of fact, in thirty-four years I never once seriously forgot my words or did anything that was disastrous for the manager or the cast who were relying upon me. But the bigger the part the greater my fear; and the Dean was a very big part indeed to learn and a great responsibility to play. Athene Seyler was extremely patient and understanding, but could not persuade me to go on with *Dandy Dick*. I retired from the scene and went home.

However, the sense of relief passed rather quicker than usual and was replaced very soon by regret and alarm. At the week-end my sister-in-law, Renée, advised me to ring up the stage manager who was a friend and find out what had transpired. She told us the script was being read by Walter Fitzgerald, an actor whom I like as a man and greatly admire as an artist. There was a moment's pause; then as I put down the receiver I said firmly, "I'd rather open on Monday night at Glasgow than see Walter Fitzgerald play that part."

A little professional jealousy can do wonders. When, half an hour later, John Perry of Tennents rang up asking if I felt better and if I would like to return to the attack, I said "Yes". I did and carried it through to success.

It is impossible for me to write of *Dandy Dick* without at the same time thinking of *The Magistrate*. The leading characters of these two Pinero farces, Mr. Posket and Dr. Jedd, Dean of St. Marvells, have so many things in common. Athene Seyler and I became devoted to the Dean during rehearsals. He seemed so very real to us; and I was sad when the time came to bring my sojourn at St. Marvells to an end and say good-bye to him.

The Magistrate was an endearing character too. But for some reason or other it was the Dean to whom I finally gave my heart. I think this was because Dr. Jedd was a more flesh and blood person than Mr. Posket. When one comes to analyse the two characters, the Magistrate is a more farcical figure, whereas the Dean belongs to true comedy, although his surrounding circumstances are farcical. Dr. Jedd always seemed to me a figure I might have met any sunny day walking across the Close of a Cathedral city. But Mr. Posket felt more like someone in a nightmare, an enormous shadow figure cast by candlelight on the nursery ceiling.

Apart from my own personal reasons for doing so, it is natural to think of these two plays together, belonging as they do to the same period of early Pinero farce, before, influenced by the Ibsen trend, he began to write the serious dramas of the *declassée* woman, such as *The Second Mrs. Tanqueray* and *The Notorious Mrs. Ebbsmith*.

At the end of our season at the Lyric, Hammersmith, we did one special week with *Dandy Dick* at Cambridge. On my first free morning I could not resist the temptation to indulge in the nostalgic pastime of going back to the scene of my childhood where so many important events had happened to me, events that had made a strong impact on my mind and imagination and that had had such far-reaching effects, mainly for unhappiness, on my adult years.

That day had a dream-like quality, as I walked along the street and saw again the stream flowing along by the kerb-side that used to fascinate me when I was small and which I always understood had been "bequeathed" by some benefactor to the City. More dream-like still to wander down Bateman Street past Paston House, of which I wrote at the beginning of this book, through the Botanical Gardens out into the Trumpington Road; and, as I went home by the river bank and the lovely Backs, to stop at the old inn by the bridge in Silver Street to which Tabram, my grandmother's coachman, had retired when he left her employ.

It all looked on the surface very much the same, despite the passage of forty years or so. And yet if one stopped to think, how different! The radio shops, the cinema advertisements, the endless stream of cars

Felix H. Man

The Author in *The Magistrate*, 1943

Donald Wolfit as King Lear, 1944

and motor-buses, the roar of an aeroplane engine overhead. Where were the landaus, the broughams, the victorias, drawn by the shining, well-groomed horses? Where was the clop-clop, clop-clop of the hooves on the cobbled streets; and the faint jingling of harness, for ever associated in my mind with early-morning waking in the nursery at the top of my grandmother's house?

Paston House is now a Catholic convent school. I rang the front-door bell, and asked the nun who answered it if I might see the house and garden. She was most hospitable and obliging and took me all over it herself. From my aunts, who had been there on previous occasions, she had learned much of the history of the house in my grandmother's time; so she was able to refresh my memory when it failed me.

The "dark, shadowy hall", as I have described it, seemed, of course, much less dark and shadowy, and the walk down it much shorter before you came to the "large drawing-room on the ground floor". And inside that drawing-room, now littered with the paraphernalia of a girls' school, the French windows looked out on to a hard tennis-court and playground where my grandmother's smooth lawn had been; and the "huge glittering chandelier" was no longer there. The "tall winding staircase . . . long mysterious corridors . . . unexpected corners" were still there. But there was nothing unexpected about them any more and all mystery had gone. My grown-up mind and the scrubbed, carbolic atmosphere of a well-run convent school had dispelled it; and, in the light of that early-spring afternoon, even the sinister figure of the once-hated nurse, dark, forbidding, towering above me on the stairs, melted away like an ugly dream. . . .

My return to the theatre was no anticlimax. In addition to the Dean (which I did also on television and radio) I played another big part famous in the history of Victorian farce: Sir John Hare's rôle of Samuel Goldfinch in *A Pair of Spectacles*. Mr. Goldfinch in his way was as successful as Mr. Posket had been and I repeated him also on television. *The Magistrate* I have done on sound radio; but I have been engaged elsewhere whenever the play has been presented on the "small screen". Fortunately, for the radio version, that talented comedienne, Avice Landon, who had always played Mrs. Posket with me, was free to give again her irresistible performance.

Altogether I remained in the entertainment world as a working actor for another six years. Apart from the engagements I have mentioned there were two other plays that stand out in relief for rather different reasons.

E

> In 'Forty-nine
> A Curlew flew,
> And there was I
> And there were you.

These four lines were written by Eleanor Farjeon in the copy she gave me of the book of *The Silver Curlew*, originally a play and produced at the Arts Theatre in December, 1949.

I have told the story of all this in detail in the recent Memoir of its author. I will therefore say no more here than that the meeting brought about by my playing in this piece was the start of a great friendship. Eleanor Farjeon and I were close friends for the next fifteen years, until she died in the June of 1965. Her name has already been mentioned and will appear from time to time in what remains of my story, because there was no department of my life in which she did not have a place, and there were few friends of mine whom she did not share. Kate O'Brien, in whose play *The Ante-Room* I had been in 1936 and whom I caught up with again thirty years later and introduced to Eleanor, wrote of her afterwards:

> "Eleanor Farjeon is indeed a gift in a million to be able to offer to and share with one's friends. Thank you with all my heart for letting me meet her . . ."

The other piece that stands out in my mind does so on three accounts: the play, the playwright and the producer. All three should take a place in the history of the theatre.

A Penny for a Song, a play of poetry and magic, is dateless and can hardly fail to be revived from time to time, if only by the repertory companies. It was the first piece by John Whiting to be seen in the commercial theatre, and it was produced at the Haymarket by Peter Brook, a director who has done so many important productions since then that I would like to record my impressions of him.

Peter is a genius. All geniuses are provoking one way or another. Peter's way is less difficult to deal with than some. His treatment of actors is unexceptionable. He is friendly, kind, patient, serene, imperturbable. Most young actors, and many older ones, would find him an inspiring man to work with. For myself, quickly exhausted and easily made anxious, I found the weeks of rehearsal kept me in a constant state of fatigue and agitation.

It could be said of Peter Brook that he neither slumbers nor sleeps, that he would not know a clock if he saw one, and that he believes that the Sabbath was made for producers. He loved "business", and over mechanical things he would tinker for hours on end with the absorption of a child. By the time we had been rehearsing a week or two he had introduced a balloon that really went up and descended again into a well, and a fire engine that actually worked and belched forth steam. This second toy, designed by Emett and afterwards used in the Festival Gardens, was my particular concern. It was absolutely enchanting to look at; but it weighed a ton and I was expected to wheel it by its handles on and off stage, up and down ramps, as if it were a little coster barrow. Peter would not take "no" for an answer to anything. Always he got his way with a smiling implacability more Eastern than Western. (He is of Russian origin.)

The most dangerous moment for you in a Peter Brook production is when he takes you out to luncheon at the Ritz. (It was the Carlton Grill in my case, but as that has now been demolished it could be any other restaurant that is expensive.)

On the second day of rehearsal Peter had told me that my performance was "magical" (an adjective then coming into vogue) and had allowed me to go straight ahead on those lines. When, four weeks later within a few days of our opening night, he asked me to go out to luncheon with him, I took it as a friendly gesture and accepted with alacrity. I like Peter Brook and I like good food.

I have never less enjoyed a luncheon. He was a charming host, but from the *hors d'œuvres* to the Camembert in his gentlest tones he destroyed everything I had done up to date with my part of Lamprett Bellboys. I was on the wrong track. I had to reorganise, to reorientate, to think again. I came out of the Carlton in a daze, feeling, as actors do on such occasions, that the end of the world had come. It had not of course. The talk, no doubt, had a stimulating effect on my performance, for in the end I think it was one of the best things I did in the theatre.

Peter Brook's word that he used so freely, "magical", could be specially applied to him. He has an inner magic, and out of that fecund mind and fantasy-filled imagination he weaves his spells. He certainly cast over Whiting's lovely play a wizardry which has never been forgotten by the few who saw it at the Haymarket, where it ran only for a short time.

As to the author of *A Penny for a Song*, John Whiting, it is tragic to think that he has already gone from us. He was a true artist, a poet as well as a playwright. In fact the poetry in all his plays too often gave them an obscureness which prevented Whiting from being a draw at the Box Office. This in the scheme of things is unimportant, but the greatest artists have to live and John Whiting did this, as many do, by script-writing for films. The one play of his that stands out as a success monetarily is *The Devils*; but that was not his own original work, but a very skilful adaptation from a book by Aldous Huxley.

I can well remember meeting Whiting for the first time, as the author of *A Penny for a Song*, in Tennent's office and I used to go out to lunch with him during rehearsals. He had a reserved manner, a shy charm. But when I met him again a few years ago in the B.B.C., where we were doing his play, *Saints Day*, he had developed tremendously. He was still quiet in manner and still very charming, but he had acquired that poise and authority that only success and an assured position can give.

The last play I appeared in for a London run was *The White Sheep of the Family*, with Jack Hulbert at the Piccadilly. I played yet another clergyman. This time he was an absent-minded vicar: a never-failing joke with English audiences.

I remember the argument about terms with the business manager. I did not know it was the last talk of its kind I should have. Never having employed an agent I always had to deal with the contracts myself. This was no doubt unwise. I was far too tentative to make a good business man; and for much of my career I worked for a figure well below what I should have received. But by the time I came to *The White Sheep of the Family* I had ceased to care any more. In fact, I would have been glad if the offer, which involved a long tour before the London run, had fallen through. The psychological effect of this uncaring attitude towards employment on a usually diffident character was remarkable. Having, after some discussion, agreed to the salary and billing I asked for, the manager said amiably "My God! You're *terrible*—and all done so quietly too. Thank God you're not an agent!"

Soon once again I was on the road. This time not in a hired car but in my own. With the end of petrol-rationing I had bought a Bond Minicar; and on an August Saturday, 1953, I started out alone in this unsuitable form of transport for Liverpool. I took thirteen hours, going twenty-five miles out of the way to avoid what were for me the terrors of the Mersey Tunnel.

I wrote at length in *Eleanor* about this tour, because Miss Farjeon and her car played a big part in it. The drives to Liverpool and Newcastle in the Minicar had proved too exhausting and she lent me her Hillman for the last five or six weeks. I arrived safely back in London and played my part at the Piccadilly for the long run; repeating it on radio and television.

When that was over, Eleanor Farjeon and I attempted a three-weeks motoring holiday in Scotland. We reached as far as Ripon and were home again in a week. I knew then I could not face any more long-distance driving.

That short adventure on the now nightmare roads and the tour of the previous year, augmented by the growing chaos of the parking problems in London, brought me face to face with a disagreeable fact. This was that the car, which had always stood for me as a symbol of freedom and personal mobility, was no longer anything of the sort. Just as I could not stop a train or bring an aeroplane down at will and get out, so now I could see myself being confined in my own car on the road, because unable to abandon it in a mile-long, bumper-to-bumper queue. In the end, in fact, I gave up keeping a car at all and have had to manage with buses out of the rush-hour, taxis and minicabs —and of course walking.

So the return of the so-called peace had done nothing to restore my morale as to mobility, with this congestion on the roads now as much as on the railways. Moreover, the conditions of modern life, the unending difficulties and frustrations, so wearing even to normal people, kept me in a constant state of apprehension. To add the anxieties of an actor's existence to all this seemed no longer practicable. The stage was a relentless enough profession before the war; but the post-war theatre suited me even less as a walk of life.

It had become tremendously decentralised and no doubt rightly. If you were successful—and who could want to remain on the stage if they were not successful?—you had to be prepared to accept everything you could possibly squeeze in in the way of theatre, television, radio and films, and go anywhere to fulfil the commitment. An actor's life was becoming yearly more and more unpeaceful. I grew increasingly restless and agitated by this hectic profession, which made such demands on nerve and body. I could still face an audience with comparative equanimity; but to stay put hour upon hour in the dressing-room backstage: that was the torment. The charm had gone long ago. Now the courage was going too.

At Easter time 1954, I was once again rehearsing on that stage at the Haymarket from which I had made my retreat seven years earlier. John Gielgud was again the producer and I was to play one of the best small parts ever written for an actor: Firs, the old coachman, in *The Cherry Orchard*. As I have written elsewhere:

"I liked the part and was already beginning to feel that sense of interior identification with the character which always made even me hopeful of success in the rôle I was playing. In a mood of fatal optimism I worked on Firs for several days; but soon the all-too familiar sense of uneasiness set in."

I pictured the poky dressing-rooms at the Lyric, Hammersmith, where we were to run for six weeks, and envisaged a network of tours at home and abroad before I could be finished with Firs and *The Cherry Orchard*.

"At four o'clock one morning, after an almost sleepless night, I decided to throw in my hand and that this time it must be for good. I wrote a letter of explanation to John Gielgud and walked down through the quiet streets to leave it and the script with the fireman at the Haymarket stage-door.

As I walked home again I realised that I had taken a fatal step, had reached the point of no returning. I wondered what lay ahead. Although I had found little happiness on the stage, acting had appeared to be my vocation all those years. With my usual probings I asked myself if I had done a weak thing in turning my back on it all at a comparatively early age. But as the time went by I was to see very clearly that all this was meant to be. I was to find that it was possible to have more than one vocation in life."

What I could not see then was that waiting round the corner was a calling which would bind me in a different way closer than ever to the theatre and to the lives and work and problems of those who were seeking the very things from which I had fled.

PART II

CHAPTER XXV

Albert Finney, Peter O'Toole, David Warner, Alan Bates, John Stride, Frank Finlay, Tom Courtenay, Richard Briers, Brian Bedford ...

It was they who were waiting round that first sharp corner; to mention only a few, the few that Fortune favoured. And not all at once, of course. One by one, two by two, they stepped forward out of the shadows from their several backgrounds.

That was a word that suddenly began to assume an importance—"background"; for how different now and how various were the social strata from which the Academy students came. Before the war, the R.A.D.A. had been a "snob" institution and most of them came from the privileged classes. But by 1954, rightly, all that was changed. Government grants to meet the fees had come into being and with a large proportion of the students the great enemy to be dealt with was "background". Even today, when so much in the way of good speech has gone by the board, the attention of stage students has to be drawn to the advisability of acquiring Standard English, or "educated" English as it used to be called, for the purposes of poetry, for Shakespeare and the other classical verse plays, and for those set against the Belgravian *milieu* of Oscar Wilde.

When I returned to the R.A.D.A. in the summer of 1954 it was these questions of Standard English and speech in general that were my chief concern. Diction the class was still called; and it was taught as a separate subject from Voice Production of which it really is a part. The teachers of Voice were men and women highly trained in the art of breath control and proper production of vocal tone. The Diction teachers of Sir Kenneth Barnes's time were experienced actors and actresses of some standing, who had learned the hard way of practical experience how to speak good English, how to articulate, how to "phrase" and how generally to manage dramatic material and deal with words.

To this I added sight-reading: a most necessary accomplishment for every actor and actress; for they can never tell when they are going to be asked to read something at sight. On such occasions they are not only expected to read intelligently and without stumbling, but also to give some idea of the character which they are to interpret. This applies especially in radio, where everything has to be read, but to be made to sound as if it were not being read.

This particular aspect of Diction naturally stresses the elements of background and education; not least in the accepted pronunciation of words.

I had found it difficult to deal with those returning from the battle-fields in 1947. It was even more bewildering when in 1954 I came to meet this still younger generation that had sprung up while my back was turned.

However this time, having once and for all got the theatre out of my system, instead of looking upon the work as just a job to be done because I could no longer do something else, I approached the teaching from a quite different and more positive point of view: a vocational one. I set out at once not only to learn to teach, for it is one thing to have knowledge and another to know how to impart it, but also to get to know and understand the New Young.

Before long, I found how much I liked them with their gaiety and enthusiasm and their quick humour; their sensitive understanding, too, of things of which I at their age had not begun to be aware. And there was much about them that stirred one's compassion, when one realised the circumstances in which many of them did their training. Some worked in pubs and coffee bars during the vacations; some were so hard-up that they had to work in the evenings during term-time; and one knew in certain cases that they were just not getting enough to eat. Perhaps I was inclined to sentimentalise it, but their courage and powers of endurance seemed touching and very much endeared them to me.

When later I wrote my first book about the ways of the stage for the beginning actor, I dedicated it to all R.A.D.A. students. I certainly owed them a debt, for unknowingly they helped me quite as much as many of them have been kind enough to say I helped them. However dark my mood when I walked round to the Academy from my flat, when I returned after concentrating on the students and their work and problems I found that the cloud had lifted.

It is not, I think, exaggerated to say that the New Young gave me back my own "youth". Had I never been to the R.A.D.A. and taught them and got to know and like them, I should no doubt today be a Scrooge-like bachelor, living in his ebony tower, the windows shut-tered against an alien world.

I was, in fact, experiencing for the first time the satisfaction of play-ing a willing and co-operative part in an organisation towards which I felt a positive loyalty; and once again, as at the Arts Theatre in 1942, of doing work for the work's sake and for little financial reward.

At the end of the first year after my return to the R.A.D.A. Sir Kenneth Barnes retired. He had done his life's work and had done it to the end with devotion, enthusiasm and single-mindedness. In the face of tremendous odds, mainly financial, he had kept the Academy going all through the war and for the ten years that followed its termination. He had launched a thousand stars—actors and actresses. He had built one theatre which was virtually wiped out by the enemy and over the rubble that remained raised up another which we now know as the Vanbrugh.

He called it by the name taken by his two illustrious actress sisters, Violet and Irene, who had brought dignity and distinction to the theatre and had always played an active part in furthering the interests of the Academy.

Kenneth Barnes had been brought up with a love of the theatre and had been connected with it from his youngest days. At one time he had been a dramatic critic. With this background and his very fine character, he was eminently suited to be the Principal of the Academy founded by Sir Herbert Tree for student actors and actresses.

As a teacher of Diction I was frequently present at mid-term diction tests conducted by the Principal. Sir Kenneth's knowledge of the rudiments of good speech was remarkable. He could always tell each student exactly where his faults lay and how to remedy them.

The Royal Academy of Dramatic Art, to give it its full title and dignity, and countless actors and actresses owe a great debt to Sir Kenneth Barnes and may that never be forgotten.

Nevertheless, the time had come to give the work over into the hands of a younger man; a man better fitted to the formidable task of adapting the Academy's needs to a changed world which had been through a second world war and a bloodless revolution. The man was there waiting: John Fernald.

Having served under both *régimes* I feel myself not unfitted to assess their respective qualifications; and I shall always consider that Fernald was the right man for that particular job at that particular moment. Old enough to be experienced and authoritative, he was also young enough to bring to the post the kind of enthusiasm which could galvanise the organisation into a school that would inspire the modern drama student seeking a very different theatre to which we had been accustomed.

Fernald always reminded me of a student himself—the eternal

student. He lived, talked, ate, drank, dreamed theatre, nothing but theatre. This was bound to have an effect on the students themselves.

He was a broom that swept clean, of course, and very clean. But most of his innovations proved themselves successful in the end. He very soon abolished the annual Public Performance which had been an Academy institution for years. It was a sort of Derby Race. There were the favourites who were given the splendid opportunities but sometimes one of the major prizes was snaffled by an outsider, some smaller part player whose talent was so obvious that the judges were compelled to take notice of them.

John Fernald discontinued this and put in its place the practice of having several afternoon and evening performances of each play in the Vanbrugh Theatre, which gave the students the experience of playing a part several times to different audiences, which was invaluable. And it gave them a greater number of opportunities of being seen under more favourable conditions by managers and agents.

Fernald also abolished the Diction classes; or rather he called them by another name. In Kenneth Barnes's time the students had only been allowed to use plain prose as opposed to dramatic dialogue. This had the advantage of making them concentrate on the words only, without being able to fall back on the emotional content to help them out. Fernald could see that, admirable though it might be in theory, it was dull and uninspiring for a theatre student. So he changed the name of my class to Audition Technique. This was a brilliant idea, because the students had all that they had had before, but in addition they felt they were being initiated into something which was eminently practical and would be of immediate use to them when they left the Academy. To be "auditioned" for almost every part he plays is the common lot of the young actor of today.

As far as I myself was concerned it was the true beginning of my new career. I began to "sit in" at professional auditions in order to pass on to the students at first hand just what was required of them on these exacting occasions. I went frequently to the regular theatre auditions held by H. M. Tennent; and later was allowed to be present at those held by the B.B.C. television, sound radio and Schools' departments.

It was this research and the work with students that resulted from it which led to my writing the first book, *Advice To A Player*, and the two others that followed upon it. I also compiled an anthology of audition pieces for actors, *Choosing Your Piece*, which of all my books for drama students has perhaps been the one in most constant use.

The first was concerned almost entirely with practical matters, such as how to go about getting jobs, how to write letters, how to study their appearance and make the best of themselves, when they had to attend an audition.

John Neville, who had been in my class in 1947, wrote a Foreword to that first book, and Albert Finney to its successor, *Acting My Way*. I have always made shameless use of my past students. Finney calls it exercising my "emotional blackmail".

CHAPTER XXVI

No DRAMA TEACHER could have been luckier than I was, in that I struck what I can only describe as the Golden Period at the R.A.D.A. Few instructors would be fortunate enough to have two "giants" in one class. At one time I had Albert Finney and Peter O'Toole in the same group. They were both with me for at least two terms, because I remember them clearly in the Diction class days; and Richard Briers too, so popular now on stage and television, endearing, restless, high-spirited, undoubtedly a born comedian.

Brian Bedford, who seems at present lost to us in America, had a brilliant talent, which showed itself afterwards in *Five Finger Exercise*, *A View From the Bridge* and in *The Tempest* with John Gielgud at Drury Lane. I picked him out immediately at a Diction Test which I took for Sir Kenneth Barnes. And John Stride (discovered as a schoolboy by Michael Croft), our best Romeo for many years; he was a "natural" for Shakespeare, with an innate gift for speaking verse. John had impeccable manners and was loved by all the staff.

Alan Bates was also unfailingly polite and easy to deal with, though something of a dark horse theatrically speaking. But within a short time of his leaving the R.A.D.A. he had got well started on his splendid career. I was soon visiting him in his dressing-room at the Royal Court after a performance of *Look Back in Anger*.

Frank Finlay, now a memorable Iago and one of Sir Laurence Olivier's favourite *protégés*, was the darkest horse of all. Beloved by everyone, he seemed older than his classmates, rather heavy, be-spectacled, always worried and frustrated. One would never have imagined him going where he has gone so fast of recent years. Now, no spectacles, a different hair style, years younger-looking and an exquisite and assured actor. *Chips with Everything*, Chichester and the National Theatre. A surprise, but what a pleasant one. Certainly contact lenses are one of science's greatest gifts to actors. Being able to dispense with glasses made all the difference to Finlay.

Tom Courtenay and David Warner came along much later. I never had any doubt about Tom. Everything he did was instinctively right and true. His strange, rather melancholy face was right, too, and seemed especially designed to fit into the contemporary theatre. And he was a worrier. I do like actors who worry; they are almost invariably the most gifted.

David Warner, our brilliant Henry VI and most discussed and disturbing Hamlet, was, I must confess, another surprise. Not that I did not always enjoy working with him, nor fail to regard him as a gifted actor in the making. But I would not have imagined his taking—and so quickly—the particular place he has in the classical theatre of today. He was to me an interesting "character" actor, but not a leading man; an actor who one would have expected to find things difficult in his early days, but to come into his own as he got older. How very differently things turned out and how happy I felt for him when I read his wealth of press notices, as he went from one success to another. Warner is another actor who has profited from being able to wear contact lenses. I remember him at the R.A.D.A. with a myopic look and wearing strong glasses.

John Neville comes into a class by himself in more ways than one. He was in my Diction group much earlier on, in 1947, when I made my first attempt to retire and must have been a feeble teacher. Neville was among the slow starters. I can see him now, standing up to do a Shakespearean speech. He had everything of voice, face and figure that an actor needs; and yet there was something then of personality missing or submerged. Later, in his Foreword to my book, he explained it, admitting to a "lack of confidence" and a "sense of failure" in his student days. But how he was to develop afterwards! When I saw him as Hamlet, giving one of my favourite performances of my favourite part, I could hardly believe I was watching the same man.

Neville is a very fine character, with high ideals for the theatre and in regard to life itself. For many years now he has felt strongly, as I do, about the colour-bar question. This he demonstrated in a very practical way. John and his wife, Caroline, adopted first a small coloured boy, then later a little coloured girl to match up with their own children.

The magnificent work he does at the Nottingham Playhouse as an actor, manager and director, is well known and he is much respected and loved by his fellow players.

To return to the two "giants" with which I began this chapter: Albert Finney and Peter O'Toole. It was no surprise to anyone that they began immediately to do well, although they were both sensible enough to go out of London and learn their job before attempting to storm the West End.

Albert Finney told me he had a Five Year Plan; and in fact he refused offers to play in London. He walked the Olivier way; to Birmingham, where he worked his passage till he was given big leading rôles, his performances of which are talked of still. He was determined to have behind him several years of repertory experience; then and then only Finney considered himself ready to face London— New York—the World.

Meanwhile, down in the West Country, Peter O'Toole was follow-ing much the same pattern at the Bristol Old Vic. But he added some-thing to his Five Year Plan: he altered his nose and his "image". I preferred both as they were before. Not that I really know him now as a private personality, as I know Finney. But at the R.A.D.A. Peter was a particularly likeable student and a stimulating one to work with; and I liked his nose, which had character and suited the face it was made to go with.

Both of them were in my Diction group for at least one term, but remained on in the new Audition Class when John Fernald took over the administration. They neither of them worked well in the first term and I am not surprised. It was a dull type of lesson and I had not yet learned to teach. Audition Technique made me feel more like a pro-ducer again; and it must have made the students conscious that they were doing something closer to the living theatre. Anyway, after that Albert Finney and Peter O'Toole always did exciting work for me.

Even in the dull Diction class days I remember noticing Finney's soft and gentle notes, which he used in the quieter narrative passages with which we were then concerned. They were a pleasure to listen to and his slight Salford accent only seemed to enrich the vocal texture. He could also produce an enormous voice and he would play up in my small classroom as if he were in Drury Lane. I remember him especially as O'Neill's Emperor Jones; and with gratitude as the only student who had the enterprise to learn the whole of the long Prologue to *A Trip to Scarborough*. It is a tremendous speech and calls for great variety and style. Albie did it with exactly the right elegance and *panache*.

Albert Finney I regard as rather an exceptional character. He has easy, charming manners, that come naturally out of a fundamentally warm and generous nature. Unfortunately considerations of secrecy make it impossible for me to write of the kind things he has done and the trouble he has taken for those less fortunate than himself. But one little example I can give of Albie's innate niceness. He and I met in a radio programme and once went out to lunch together. Owing to my allergy to elevators I always have to climb the B.B.C. staircase to studio 8 on the top floor where we were rehearsing. After lunch, as Albie and I reached the lift doors, I waved and said, "See you later", and made for the stairs. "Oh no," said Albert, "I'll walk with you."

And he did. Could there be a better example of good manners and sensitiveness? Yet, there are disgruntled, middle-aged people who are always running down the present young.

I had this endearing letter from Albie, when I wrote to congratulate him on the birth of his son. He was then making his first London appearance, with Charles Laughton.

New Theatre
Thursday evening

Dear Mr. Blakelock,

Many thanks for your note; it was very kind of you. Simon is a great kid; very clever he is. His Voice Production is already better than his Dad's; and he's very clever with his eyes.

A friend of ours had a dream that he would be the greatest billiard player that ever was. That's snookered my dreams of his being a great actor.

I adored your book, by the way, Mr. Blakelock. All the information in it is very useful. I remember, for instance, my first visit to an agent's office. It's much worse than stage nerves because one's really on one's own.

It was at M.C.A. and I was ushered into this carpeted, gilded, marble-staircased palace and shown into a large office. Almost the first thing the agent said to me was, "Hm-m. We'll have to stick that right ear back for films." Nearly died.

You see, I think a book like yours is really more use than books of Methods of Acting, etc., as acting is a personal thing. One can help someone to mould their talent and shape it; but one can't really tell them what it's made of.

What can be really explained are the actor's social requisites, which you do so well. How to write the letters, etc., all simply and clearly explained. Very good it is.

Thanks again for letter.

Love
Albie

Now for the moment I must leave all these talented actors it was my good luck to teach—and to be taught by. I should like to end this chapter, however, by expressing my regret that when one comes to write this kind of book one can only discourse upon the happy few.

There are the unhappy many: the frustrated, the unrecognised, the unfulfilled for one reason or another, despite their early promise and their undoubted gifts. I think with affection of them: the vast numbers of student-actors at the R.A.D.A. who passed through my hands and who are not forgotten; on the contrary, whose work and talents and friendship will be always remembered with gratitude and appreciation.

These verses, which I wrote for an R.A.D.A. magazine, are perhaps most of all for them. I wrote them after a staff meeting in the empty Academy building:

> The term is over,
> The lessons stored away;
> All those bright faces now are gone
> Into the outer world,
> Faces with radiant expectancy that shone,
> Or clouded with resentment and dismay.
>
> The noise has died,
> The footsteps one by one have clattered
> And then ceased;
> The voices that for a term have chattered
> Now are fallen into silence;
> The students now are scattered
> Far and wide.
>
> On the staircase,
> Up and down, the quickly moving figures
> Seem to tread in our imagining,
> Then vanish down the echoing corridor;
> Memory moves
> Towards those whose gifts and graces
> Gave us the hope that spring
> Holds in its store;
> For them we wish a fruitful summer,
> A golden autumn; to us remaining
> They will return no more.

CHAPTER XXVII

ALL THAT I have described really *was* going on "round the corner"; because living where I did I only had to turn the corner into Tavistock Square, walk across Gordon Square, down Torrington Place and I was in Gower Street and at the R.A.D.A.

But in addition to this and running side by side with it there were teaching activities building up for which I did not even have to turn the corner. I used my own flat as a studio, where I took a steadily increasing number of pupils who came for private lessons.

These were not only theatre students; but people of every kind and nationality, wanting help with their English or with various aspects of self-presentation and public speaking. If I could not say they were Parthians and Medes and Elamites, or dwellers in Mesopotamia and Cappadocia and the parts of Libya about Cyrene, I could with truth state that from the Arabian desert and Africa they came; from Australia, New Zealand and the Americas; from Iraq, Iran, Israel and from India and the Far East. Not to mention Oswestry, Bolton and dwellers in the parts of London about Hornsey Rise.

Actors and actresses, priests and Rabbis, law-students and medicos; Cabinet Ministers and company directors; soldiers and sailors, debs and beatniks; backward boys, forward girls and pop-singers. Looking back over the twelve years since my teaching life began in earnest the picture I have painted is no exaggeration; and that side of it was really the more interesting of the two. I mean that, having lived a rather insular life, to meet such a number of people from so many other lands and to listen to their problems was an education in itself for me and gave me a sense of purpose. I still had the many actors and actresses and theatre aspirants, for whom I had a special affection of course; though I could have wished there were not quite so many "Mrs. Worthingtons" wanting to put their daughters on the stage; or quite so many sadly untalented young people trying to escape from the humdrum of life, behind that Magic Door which once had seemed so glamorous to me.

My greatest difficulty was to decide when to come out into the open and tell them as kindly as possible that in my opinion they did not possess the necessary gifts. One really charming girl, when I told her this, took it very well at first, but ten minutes later began to cry and could not stop. I had to give her lunch and try to comfort her for at least two hours. After that I vowed I would never take the risk again. But of course I did, because honesty compelled me; and in one such instance the pupil rang up the next morning demanding her money back, which she received. So a drama coach's life is not a happy one—always. But on the whole my experience of human nature through this work has been very pleasant; and my liking for my fellow beings has been greatly increased as a result of it.

Of all my private teaching "cases" Mr. X, the Cabinet Minister, was one of the most interesting and one that of its very nature led me a little way into a world that had always seemed far from my accustomed paths.

It is impossible to write much of this, concerning as it does a man in a very responsible position. Even to deal with it anonymously could easily lead people to put two and two together and uncover the identity of Mr. X.

He was sent to me, or I to him, through the medium of the Academy and his reason for coming was obvious. He wanted a speech-trainer's help in making his diction clear and interesting in the House of Commons.

After an initial interview at the Ministry he agreed, busy man though he was, to come for lessons to my flat, where I had my text books, my tape-recorder and all the clobber of my trade. In his case, of course, I had to give him preference in the matter of appointments and to be prepared to watch his public appearances on television. It also led to my going several times to hear him speak in the House and on one occasion to an important Exhibition he was opening and to the luncheon afterwards where he made a speech.

As we came to know each other better, I was invited more than once to dinner at his flat and taken to dine also in the House of Commons. There I had the pleasant experience of walking along the famous terrace by the river, where I was able to pick out faces that I knew well by sight.

Each Cabinet Minister has a room of his own in the House of Commons, in addition to his office at the Ministry. After we came in from the terrace Mr. X. took me down to this room of his, where we had a little more conversation. Ten minutes later, feeling like an F.B.I. man, I was being let out by a policeman through a secret door.

One of my pupils who brought great joy into our household was the Japanese film star, Yoko Tani, who has given me permission to mention her name.

She was sent to me by Robin Midgley, producer of Hal Porter's *The Professor*, at the Royal Court, in which she was appearing. We had many sessions together in order to help her with the language difficulty.

Japanese women have always seemed to me to have a peculiar beauty and there was no disillusion to be found in Yoko Tani. We became real friends; and now, whether she is in her flat in Rome, or flying about in the Far East, she always sends me affectionate cards of greeting. Only the other day she was in London for a television programme and she came to see us with an armful of beautiful chrysanthemums.

I learned something amusing and interesting from Yoko on that occasion. Her life is built round her toy dogs—"my boy and my girl". Recently the "boy" appeared to be pregnant. The vet examined him and said it was an "imaginative" pregnancy—Yoko's word.

"Phantom" babies are quite usual in medical practice, and there is a case well known in psychology of a boy about fifteen who so identified himself with his mother that he produced all the symptoms of pregnancy up to the last moment. But Yoko Tani's dog "boy" is the first case of phantom pregnancy I have come across in the animal world.

It will be seen, therefore, that in teaching many people from many lands there are also many lessons to be learned for oneself.

In my formidable list of heterogeneous pupils I mentioned pop-singers. In fact, there have been only two: one as yet not known, whom one day I hope will be, the other very well known indeed. I anticipated that he might prefer me not to reveal his name. But out of the blue from Blackpool, where he was doing a Summer Season, he telephoned and generously gave me permission to do so. The name is Adam Faith.

His arrival for the initial lesson, I learned afterwards, caused considerable fluttering within the dovecotes of our block of flats, as the quietly dressed figure of Variety's Golden Boy slid out of the driving seat of the discreet grey Rolls.

For his first visit we gave him the full treatment, accorded only to V.I.P.'s. My sister-in-law, Renée, looking more stylish than the smartest Harley Street receptionist, opened the door to him and, as Adam Faith walked into the room, I rose from my bureau as though occupied with a wealth of business affairs.

His second appointment happened to coincide with the visit of my Mrs. Hibbert from Chelsea, who comes once a week to give the flat *her* full treatment—a "thorough do". Mrs. Hibbert is an ardent pop-singer fan. There is nothing she cannot tell you about each one of them. I was determined to give her a real surprise. That afternoon I told her I was expecting a rather special pupil and asked her to oblige me by answering the bell when he rang.

I would have given much to have been at the front door when Mrs. Hibbert opened it to find herself face to face with Adam Faith. When I slipped out into the kitchen a few moments later she was still recovering from the shock.

Adam Faith came to me because he wanted to "go on to other things", he told me. He would have in mind films, mainly, and even the theatre; and, just as Albert Finney and Peter O'Toole and John Neville all worked on their speech and voice, even after they left the R.A.D.A., so Adam realised he could do with a little help. He is supremely intelligent; that handsome head of his is packed with shrewd commonsense and the large blue eyes miss nothing of what passes before them. The charm and the flashing smile, so well-known to millions, are sparingly used outside of his professional work. This gives him an air of sincerity and honest straightforwardness that only makes him the more likeable and commands one's respect.

That Adam Faith has plenty of character was revealed in a story he told me of his boyhood. At the age of twelve he owed £100 for the Hire Purchase of a bicycle and his record-player, the form having been signed by his father. He lost no time in paying back the money by earning it: doing a newspaper round and odd jobs for his mother in the offices of the firm for which she worked. Adam was off for a summer season and could only come to me for about a dozen sessions. This was not nearly long enough to do what we wanted, but it was better than nothing.

These Big Names in the Variety world are surrounded by a body-guard of agents, secretaries and "road-managers". Adam spoke to me once on the telephone. Otherwise it was invariably his agent, Eve Taylor, on the line. I shall always remember her closing remark when she had finally rung up to fix the appointments for Adam:

"And if he's not talking like Sir Laurence Olivier in three weeks I'll want to know the reason why!"

The most highly-coloured and dramatic episode of my teaching years was the one connected with Alice. That was not her real name of course, but she looked like Alice: the same age and height and size; and her hair was done in the way always connected with Lewis Carroll's

small girl. I think my Alice was a little older, but she was well below
the age of consent and that plays an important part in the story.

Alice had been to a drama school where they specialised in children.
Their chief speciality, apparently, was the "improvement" of their
pupils' speech. I put the word in quotation marks because Alice, who
had had a strong northern accent, by the time she reached me had
acquired a painfully "refined" way of talking. This it was my intention
to attempt to smooth out; also to give her a little dramatic coaching
preparatory to her being a professional actress when she was older.

Alice was brought to me by an elderly theatrical manager; we will
call him Mr. Wolf. He told me he was acting on her parents' behalf.
He had met them in the provinces and, finding that Alice wanted to be
a child-actress, he had given her the name part in his Christmas
pantomime—Little Red Riding Hood.

This had been over for some weeks, but Mr. Wolf was still interesting himself in Alice's theatrical career. He brought her each day, waited
an hour for her, and paid for the fees on behalf of the child's parents.
He also had a coaching session for himself; this too I was told to put
down to their account. That was Mr. Wolf's first false move, as it
added to certain suspicions which were beginning to form in my mind.

These misgivings had begun with strange talk of a play in which he
himself was rehearsing Alice each day after they left me. He even
outlined the theme—a not original story of sadism and seduction. This
was unwise of Mr. Wolf. Perhaps he supposed me to be a possible
accomplice? Or a man too innocent to be aware of the undertones?
In either supposition he was mistaken.

It was unfortunate for Mr. Wolf that I have always had a "rescuing"
fantasy. There is nothing I like better than playing the Scarlet
Pimpernel off-stage, because I have never been allowed to play him on.

At 10.15 on the morning following Mr. Wolf's revelations I was
expecting Alice for another lesson. At eight o'clock, before my
solicitor-cousin could leave his home, I rang him to find out exactly
how I stood in regard to libel and defamation of character. "You are
completely covered by the Law," was his reply, "if you are dealing
with a minor." I *was* dealing with a minor and I determined to deal
with the matter in a major way.

When Alice turned up for her lesson I was all prepared. "Let's just
talk for a little and see how your speech is getting on, shall we?" As I
said this I turned on my most avuncular smile. I also turned on the
tape-recorder.

The sight of the turntable going round went to my head. I changed at that moment from the Scarlet Pimpernel into the most up-to-date secret agent. James Bond? I could see myself as the heroic figure in the court scene, with the judge listening intently to the irrefutable recorded evidence of my conversation with the child. I then proceeded with the lesson on the usual lines, getting Alice to talk about herself, her parents and her home; above all finding out her father's name and full address. I also led her on to tell me something about the play in which she was being rehearsed by Mr. Wolf, she told me, in a room in the region of Leicester Square. There was apparently no script. He "made up" the words as he went along. The plot was plain, full of action, melodramatic, undoubtedly sinister.

Sitting there telling me all I needed to know, Alice looked as innocent as her namesake. I was thankful to realise that the Scarlet Pimpernel had arrived in time.

That day I wrote to her father, a shopkeeper in the north. The letter was careful but left no room for misunderstanding. Early the following morning he telephoned to me; at three o'clock in the afternoon the child's parents were in my flat; and on the evening express northwards Little Red Riding Hood was being rushed to home and safety, leaving the Big Bad Wolf to gnash his teeth at me in vain.

CHAPTER XXVIII

By 1954, when I finally exchanged an actor's life for a teacher's, my friendship with Eleanor Farjeon had got well under way. Every weekend and much of the spare week time too was spent up at her house or in her garden in Hampstead.

Through her, new interests came flooding in and new friendships were made. Over the fifteen years before she died in 1965, my education, so sadly neglected, was advanced beyond description and my whole attitude to life was subtly influenced. Not that Eleanor Farjeon was the kind of woman who set out to "improve" other people; but it was just not possible to live so much of one's life in the company of such a remarkable character without inevitably being changed.

It was through her and at her house that I turned the most unexpected corner of all; to find something which was to have important repercussions on my new work as a teacher and on myself as a human being.

On the Sunday of the same week that I made my decision to leave the stage I did my first piece of serious writing. That it should be writing was not in itself so surprising, as I had previously made an abortive attempt to produce a book of reminiscences, though I had long ago abandoned it. The surprise was that what I wrote that Easter Sunday was poetry—two poems. This was a form of creative activity that I had never dreamed of. But from then onwards verses of every kind poured out of me like a cataract.

At first with my history they were insistently religious, morbid and laden with guilt: a vomiting forth of all the poisons that had gathered in my unconscious over fifty troubled years. But my poetry-writing took exactly the same course as my life as an actor had done. Just as I had begun with a passion for playing emotional parts and had been proved in the end to be at my best as a comedian, so as a writer of verse I soon worked my way through the intense and tragic phase and found some success with the satirical poem and the *vers de société*.

In three years from that Sunday I had had a long "sick" poem accepted by John Hadfield for *The Saturday Book* and illustrated by Ronald Searle. As it concerned itself with psychological terms and the names of drugs it appealed to the American market. It was published in *Demoiselle* and made more money for me proportionately than anything I have written.

It was fortunate for me that at the time I began to write I was in constant touch with Father Lucius McClean, then editor of the Assisi Press of Dublin. He not only printed two early narrative poems, but also published two "slim volumes" of collected verse. For these, of course, I found the money. I had no illusion about my poetry and knew only too well how slender were the chances of persuading any firm to do them.

However, they have justified themselves. Ernest Milton did a group of them for a Catholic Stage Guild poetry-reading and with his vocal magic made them sound far better than they were. On another similar occasion Mary O'Farrell read two poems from *The Chastening* most beautifully; and Alan Rye brought just the right sincerity to *Jesus Was A Countryman*.

Of the poets, Christopher Hassall was kindest to me, generous, encouraging and constructive. Shortly before his sadly premature death I sent him an experimental poem, *Dives and Lazarus 1962*, which I reproduce here, together with the letter he wrote to me about it.

DIVES AND LAZARUS 1962

Dives, Dives,
Where is it you're living?
Park Lane? . . . Penthouse?
Have you no misgiving?

Dives, Dives,
What is that you're clad in?
Purple and fine linen;
It's perfect to be bad in.

Dives, Dives,
Purple and fine linen?
Yes, you know it's splendid
For living deep in sin in.

Dives, Dives,
What is that you're eating?
Avocados . . . caviare;
They take a lot of beating.

Dives, Dives,
What is that you say?
That I fare sumptuously
Every blessèd day.

★   ★   ★

Lazarus, Lazarus,
Where are you lying?
Huddled in the doorway,
His only thought of dying.

Lazarus, Lazarus,
What do you lie clad in?
Paper, rags and sacking;
They do me—to be sad in.

Lazarus, Lazarus,
What is that you're munching?
Potato peel . . . broken crusts;
They take a bit of crunching.

Lazarus, Lazarus,
What is that you say?
That I fare frugally
Every cursèd day.

★   ★   ★

Dives, Dives,
Look across the Park there;
Vagrants, bums and down-and-outs,
Sitting in the dark there.

Dives, Dives,
Are you without pity?
Oblivious of the lonely,
With no abiding city?

Dives, Dives,
Lazarus, in your doorway,
Lacks food, lacks clothes;
A chance is coming your way.

Dives, Dives
Is your heart of stone, there?
No, it feels for one man;
Me, myself alone, here.

Dives, Dives,
Death may come—it's true, now;
That is taken care of,
I'm as good as you, now.

Lazarus, Lazarus,
Death will come for you.
Let it come and welcome;
God have mercy, do.

★   ★   ★

Lazarus and Dives,
Both are gone away now;
Lazarus, be happy,
In Abraham's bosom stay now.

Dives, where's the penthouse?
Where the sumptuous living?
The purple, the fine linen
You found so good to sin in?

Dives, Dives,
Now you lie and languish,
For never loving Lazarus,
When he lay in anguish.

★   ★   ★

Lazarus prays for Dives,
From his place of peace;
That tortured though he be,
His torments soon may cease;

Learning that a heart of flesh,
Compassion and sweet giving,
Mean more than all the sumptuousness,
The purple, the fine linen.

Tonford Manor
Canterbury,
Kent

December 10th
1962

My dear Denys,

It was nice hearing from you. And I was delighted to have the poem. It is a curious and, I think, wholly successful, blend of the archaic and the direct-between-the-eyes modern. I'm sure devotional verse should be like that nowadays and I like "compassion and sweet giving", the mixture of naïveté and rather stark sophistication is most effective.

I've done a religious poem in a sequence of forty sonnets, which Longman will publish some time next year. It's an Elegy, in effect, for Frances Cornford, though I do not avow that in the text. You might like parts of it, even although it's so C. of E. It is at least Christian; a rare thing nowadays. I think this ballad style of yours is very forceful.

The book on R.B. [Rupert Brooke] won't appear until about November '63. It's huge, I'm afraid, like the E.M. one [Edward Marsh]. I'm glad you went to the Edith-Me recital [Edith Evans]. She was a bit nervous. So was I!

Yours affectionately,
Christopher

One more poem in *The Saturday Book*, *The Huntswoman*, this time illustrated by Thelwell of *Punch*; and that comprises my poet's life.

I very seldom write verses now. It seems to have served its purpose, this poetry-writing phase, and to be needed no more.

CHAPTER XXIX

THE INFLUENCE OF Eleanor Farjeon, of course, had been strong in all this. Her liberal-minded attitude, like Christopher Hassall's, towards verse of all kinds was a constant encouragement and her long professional experience was unreservedly at my disposal.

Whatever may have been the merits or demerits of my poetry it did one very valuable thing for me, which became clear when I returned to the attack of trying to produce an autobiography. The continual wrestling to get a few lines of verse just right; the self-discipline needed and the economy; the painstaking choice of each word to suggest the exact meaning; the packing of the content within the compass of a small poem—all this greatly improved my prose.

Anyhow, in 1958 I had a short autobiography accepted by Tom Burns of Hollis and Carter. It was well received and though now out of print is still being read and liked in the libraries. Its market was necessarily limited, as its title and sub-title suggest—*Finding My Way: A Spiritual Journey*. Although it had a Foreword by Sir Laurence Olivier it had very little to do with the theatre; but was mainly concerned with spiritual struggles before and after my conversion to Catholicism.

One thing I very soon discovered when I came to write is that other people can't read. A very intelligent theatre friend of mine, after finishing *Finding My Way*, accused me of the statement that all actors and actresses went to Hell! This, because I had told, ironically, the story of Cardinal Manning warning Mary Anderson that if she wanted to go to Heaven she must "leave the stage". Obviously, this Calvinistic piece of spiritual advice was the Cardinal's not mine. It certainly was very un-Catholic.

Not long before the publication of the autobiography, I had had my first book published by William Heinemann, *Advice To A Player*. Experience of teaching drama students suggested to me that there were so many things they were not told, which I, as an actor, knew would be useful for them to know, before they went out into the hard, cold world beyond the Academy campus: practical things, as I have said, such as job-hunting, letter writing, stage and radio audition procedure and the study of self-presentation and personal appearance.

I hit on the idea of writing a book on these subjects in the form of letters to an imaginary student-actor called Walter Plinge. This is a name which would convey little to those outside the theatre world but should mean a great deal to anyone within it. For Walter Plinge was brought to birth, as will be shown, within a stone's throw of the Lyceum Theatre and while a rehearsal of the famous Benson Company was in process. Plinge has been the familiar friend of the actor for sixty odd years. The name of this non-existent and yet, to me, very real person has been used by stage people over and over again, when they have had to "double", that is to play two characters, and have needed a second name to conceal their identity in the lesser rôle.

This breezy letter from Sir Donald Wolfit will show exactly the part played by Walter Plinge in the professional lives of those actors especially who graduated in the Shakespearean Companies like the one in which Walter was born.

My dear Denys,

I have your note—sorry for delay—frantic broadcasts—travel to fresh air—country scents—hens to feed—and geese—early to bed— no time! Will continue as Jingle—so easy to write. Walter Plinge— used his name *many* times on my programmes—Charles Doran used him for one of my *own doubles* on my first Shakespeare tour—Strange fellow—reputed to be landlord of a pub near where Sir Frank Benson rehearsed—company always excusing themselves at rehearsal saying—"I must be absent for a little while—have urgent appointment with Walter Plinge"—frequent excursions to Plinge delayed rehearsals—In the end Benson said that "Walter Plinge must join the company—then they would be able to get on". Can't verify this story absolutely but believe it is near truth—the other version that Plinge was an *entirely* fictitious character invented for some purpose does not ring as true to me.

Yours as ever,
Donald

That Plinge was certainly not a merely fictitious character has since been finally proved by an old letter from H. O. Nicholson to *The Daily Telegraph*, lent me by his sister Nora Nicholson, that small woman of great talents so well known and loved by theatre and television audiences, as well as by her fellow artists.

Here is the letter which amounts to a kind of birth certificate of Walter Plinge:

AN OVERWORKED ACTOR
Origin of Mr. Plinge

To the Editor of "The Daily Telegraph"

Sir—May I supplement a statement by Peterborough in "The Daily Telegraph" concerning that popular actor "Mr. Walter Plinge"? The real history of his origin is this:

During Sir Frank Benson's season at the Lyceum at the beginning of 1900, the male members of the company used to repair for their midday snack to the Old Bell in Exeter Street. During the war, it may be recalled, the house was severely damaged in an air raid.

One morning I dashed into the Old Bell for a hasty drink, and having forgotten the proprietor's name, on the spur of the moment called him by the first name that came on my tongue—Mr. Plinge! The genial landlord was so taken with his new soubriquet that he cheerfully answered to it ever after.

The name Plinge, with the prefix of Walter, eventually worked its way into the Benson Company, and figured in every case requiring a "double". It was quickly adopted by other companies, with the result that Mr. Walter Plinge is at the present time one of the few actors never out of an engagement.

Yours, etc.,
H. O. Nicholson

J. C. Trewin, dramatic critic and theatre historian, has drawn my attention to the fact that, as recently as 1956, Robert Morley used the name Walter Plinge in the part he doubled—one of the brothers—in Gerald Savory's play, *A Likely Tale*, at the Globe Theatre.

So though Plinge cannot be said in these difficult days to be "never out of an engagement", he is still on the agents' books and still in the managers' minds.

He was in my mind, too, when I set out to write my first series of letters to the young actor. Addressing him as "Dear Walter" and writing in this particular way enabled me to be flexible, informal, affectionate, mildly leg-pulling—the only way in my opinion to put over instruction to young people. That is no doubt why John Fernald decided to give *Advice To A Player* as a parting gift to R.A.D.A. students, in place of a mysterious LITTLE BLACK BOOK which they had previously received on leaving. I say "mysterious" because there was some doubt as to its authorship or origin, the main subject matter being unsigned. So the LITTLE BLACK BOOK was laid aside and replaced by mine which, whatever its literary shortcomings, was extremely up-to-date as to the advice and information it contained.

It would be mock-modesty on my part for me to pretend that this small book has not been continuously successful. Quite recently, in a letter I had from Vanessa Redgrave, she said, "I in turn have always wanted to tell you that I read the first of your acting books when I was a drama student and found it enormously helpful..." And a gifted young actor, Martin Jarvis, told me one day in the B.B.C. that he had read *Advice To A Player* when he left the Academy; "And," he said, "I did everything you suggested—and it worked!"

The many similar examples I could quote have naturally been encouraging, making the labour involved in writing the book infinitely worth while, and more than compensating for the small royalties which such a work brings in.

But there was to be a less happy sequel to this innovation of John Fernald's. Within a year or so of his resignation from the R.A.D.A., it came to my ears that the book was no longer being given as a farewell gift to the students. I had little known that Fernald's decision to use *Advice To A Player* for that purpose had proved a source of displeasure to the Council when it was brought to their notice. The LITTLE BLACK BOOK, which had been dismissed in favour of mine, turned out to have been written by no less a person than Bernard Shaw himself. Moreover, the vast sums of money bequeathed by him to the R.A.D.A. must have paid for its printing hundreds of times over.

When I learned this I gave up any question of fighting for the restitution of my humble work. I am not by nature competitive; and I should never anyway attempt to compete with George Bernard Shaw.

F

CHAPTER XXX

Dear Walter Plinge,

I hear that you are about to enter into another correspondence with an old teacher of mine; so I thought I would drop you a line or two in order to give a few reasons as to why you should read his letters properly.

I find it a very difficult thing as yet, either to talk or write about acting, because for myself, in spite of it being a shared art, the creative processes within me are rather personal and private. Even so, there are branches of acting which can be moulded and shaped by teachers and friends who care. . . .

So good luck and I hope D.B.'s letters are as helpful to you as his teaching was to me.

Regards,
Albert Finney.

THIS IS AN extract from the Foreword written by Albert Finney to *Acting My Way*, the next drama book I wrote six years after the first batch of Letters to a Young Actor and as a companion volume to them. It was written in the same style and intended to help Plinge the player as opposed to Plinge the student. It was a maturer book. This short paragraph from the first letter will show what I was driving at:

"What I want to do in these letters is to go on from the purely practical, rather 'careerist' subjects of *Advice To A Player*, to write something of larger and more important matters to do with acting, which could affect various aspects of your work from the beginning; and more and more as you travel farther along the actor's way . . ."

What may be of interest to the reader of this present book is not the contents of *Acting My Way* or the fact that it was as successful as its predecessor, but the manner in which it was published and the adventures I went through in the process. Another corner turned; another part played.

Having written this new book, I offered it, as a matter of course, to the firm who had launched the first one. Unfortunately they decided against publishing it. This was fair enough but in the circumstances it left me in a difficult position. How could I expect anyone to do this second book, while its companion was still being sold by a fellow publisher? I knew I could not.

Now there is another side to my character, whom Eleanor Farjeon and I used to call Mr. Playgent. In my Memoir of her I described him in detail:

"Mr. Playgent could be as daring and determined as his counterpart was diffident and easily discouraged. Mr. Playgent was a planner, pursuing his small aims and ambitions with all the concentration of a Big Business man; looking always several moves ahead with the eye of a master chess player."

Could Mr. Playgent be perhaps the peacock I have mentioned, that the sparrow always wanted to be?

Anyhow, in the matter of *Acting My Way* Mr. Playgent's pertinacity was aroused. If no firm could be found to do my book then I would do it myself. That would be my next rôle. I would be a PUBLISHER. My customary urgency took command and I set my machinations in motion without delay.

My life seems to be largely concerned with corners. Virtually round the corner from where I live there is The Favil Press to which I had been introduced by Eleanor Farjeon many years before. I knew them as beautiful printers as she always had her elegant Christmas cards done there.

The Managing Director, Mr. A. E. Lowy, now retired, had impressed himself upon me on the telephone over the years for two reasons. First on account of his unusually pleasant voice; secondly because just as—according to a proof-reader friend—I am the only writer he knows of to have ended a book with a comma,* so Mr. Lowy is probably the only man in the world to answer the telephone on a downward inflection. "The Favil Press": he would say on picking up the receiver, and made a final statement. Whereas the rest of the world would reply on an upward inflection: "The Favil Press?" implying an added "Yes?" on a note of expectation.

However, the expectation was with me that afternoon, as I hurried round to Kensington Church Street to see him for the first time; and I found the face fitted the voice and the manner fitted both. Mr. Lowy and the whole Favil Press, its exterior and its interior and the

* The Postscript to the last letter in *Advice To A Player* ends: "You take up your pen . . . think for a moment . . . and then you begin, 'Dear Walter Plinge,' "

atmosphere created by the staff, had a charming old-fashioned air that spoke of pleasanter days. And all this combined with great efficiency and a high standard of work sent out.

I told my tale to Mr. Lowy that day and asked him what the chances were of having the book printed by him, paid for and put out by me? How much would it cost? How could I distribute it? What were the trading laws? Was I allowed to do it from my flat?

To my relief he told me that The Favil Press, although it had not the machinery for extensive publication, was in fact a publishing firm and that the distribution could be done from there. As to the costs, he would have to give me various estimates.

I went home that afternoon in a high state of excitement. It was many years now since the wistful sparrow had longed to spread his tail like the peacock; and here he was doing it—in a very small way of course. But it was an adventure and I looked forward impatiently to hearing from Mr. Lowy.

The estimates came and were not prohibitive, although to have the book done in boards was out of the question. I settled for a paperback with a laminated (shiny) outside and for an edition of 1,500. Mr. Lowy tried to save my pocket at every turn; buying at a low price an odd "lot" of superior-looking paper, which, with his printing and Geoffrey Culliford's arresting cover, helped to produce a little book of which anyone could have been proud.

The months passed by and I had the enjoyment of seeing the book through all its stages. From time to time, Mr. Lowy would take me through to those intriguing regions at the back where the real printing work went on. I was introduced to the friendly staff, to the men and to their machines; and I saw my own writings revolving on these mysterious monsters.

Meanwhile my other self, Mr. Playgent, had not been idle. On the contrary, I had plotted and planned and collected every bit of information I could find. Lists of theatre-minded booksellers in London and the Provinces, Drama Departments of Universities, names and addresses of periodicals interested in speech and acting. All these were to receive, at the right moment, one of the five hundred shiny, buttercup-yellow "announcement" cards, giving details about the book, also printed by the Favil. Not to mention the stage-director of every repertory theatre in England, with a personal note on the back asking if the card could be pinned up on the notice-board. Nothing of this kind that could be done in advance of the moment when I could pounce was left undone. The Spotlight Casting Directory, with their

Paul Scofield as Mercutio, 1947

Angus McBean

Albert Finney as
Luther in 1961

Sandra Lousada

Zöe Dominic

and as Jean in *Miss Julie*, 1966

unfailing courtesy and friendliness, promised to display the book on their counter, taking no percentage or payment for the services involved.

At last we were ready. February 24th. Publication day.

We had a little celebration party. After The Favil Press had closed its doors they came round to my flat: Mr. and Mrs. Lowy, Geoffrey Culliford and his wife and Ruth Collins who had been such a good friend to me all through.

Mr. Playgent had the ball in his hands. Albert Finney's new film was just coming out and Metro-Goldwyn-Mayer tied up the Finney Foreword—Past Teacher angle of *Acting My Way* in their advance publicity. This was worth its weight in Metro Gold to me. I received little snippets from provincial and regional newspapers throughout the country. Even so, and despite all Mr. Playgent's untiring efforts, the book could not sell in sufficient numbers to bring me back my costs. It has a limited market and it is a poor student-actor market at that. Moreover, we charged initially 12s. 6d. for it, which was too high for a paperback and for its particular buyer. It was quickly reduced to 6s.

Nevertheless, it had as good reviews as its predecessor's and it has been a help to many young actors and actresses; and it led, through my friend Alfred Rogers of Foyles' drama department, to their asking me to contribute to their Career Handbooks. Foyles have also given me on three occasions a window-display in Charing Cross Road.

When Mr. Lowy retired and The Favil Press changed hands, the distribution of *Acting My Way* became my responsibility. In the first two weeks I had orders for copies of the book from regions as widely separated as Oxfordshire, Malta, California and New Zealand. So, taking it all in all, I regard my excursion into the publishing business as a great adventure and a small success.

CHAPTER XXXI

In the autumn of 1963, just when I was feeling I had nothing more to write about, it suddenly occurred to me that there was I, in constant daily touch with Eleanor Farjeon; that she was a woman who would make a splendid subject for a biographical sketch; and that she was somebody whom a great number of people would like to know more about. I realised that there might be many writers of distinction better qualified than myself to do this, but I knew there could be no one with the intimate knowledge I possessed of her life and work and character, after fourteen years of close friendship.

I began with a very small book, little more than a monograph, a sketch, which might, even if never printed, be of use one day to someone else who would be glad of the material. I did not tell Eleanor Farjeon I was writing it.

The first draft was a failure. I showed it to Grace Hogarth, Editor of Constable's Children's Department and a great friend of Eleanor's. She was very honest; she didn't like it. I saw why and put it away. But a year later I took up the manuscript again and began to re-write. This time I told Eleanor and as it took its course she became interested, although she said she was against reading any of it as she did not like seeing herself in the looking-glass. She also did not want it published till after her death.

The crucial moment came when I found by chance a wallet of Eleanor's letters that I had kept. No wonder I had done so; they were really very important and have since been described as "containing some of the best spiritual writing seen for years". I told Eleanor of my find and she said, "You had better have your side of the correspondence." On my next visit to Hampstead she put into my hands two small satchels containing about forty letters.

This put me in a very different position. As I had Eleanor Farjeon's permission to use anything I needed I immediately set out to write quite another book. I told her how it was going all the time, and that even the typists that came liked the book and particularly her letters. In the end she said to me one day, "It's funny, isn't it? I seem to have trained you up to be my biographer."

But by then it was 1965 and she was going sadly down towards her end. I had little thought when I began it how soon the book would have to be rounded off. About a month before she died Eleanor Farjeon sent me a letter to give after her death to a literary friend and adviser in whose taste and integrity she had complete confidence. In it she asked him to read the Memoir, saying that she and I relied on him to give me his "full judgement".

This was typical of Eleanor's shrewdness and wisdom and of her tact in delicate matters. By writing that letter she was, without hurting my feelings, protecting herself and me from any un-wisdom on my part. Fortunately the friend to whom she had appealed liked the book and said that he was "completely confident that Eleanor herself would have given it her approval and her blessing".

A little later Rumer Godden, too, read the book in typescript. She was enthusiastic about it, thought it "important" and that it should be published. At the same time she had certain reservations and told me honestly that, in her opinion, *Eleanor* should not be sent out exactly as it was at that moment. Might she come and see me and make one or two suggestions?

This was a kind and generous offer, as Rumer Godden is a very busy woman, and it was invaluable to me to have the practical advice of an artist and a craftswoman of her calibre. The time we spent together over the manuscript of *Eleanor* will never be forgotten. I learned more about professional writing and shaping a book and editing letters in those two hours than I had been able to discover for myself in ten years of inexpert scribbling.

So before very long *Eleanor: Portrait of a Farjeon* was ready to be sent out. This time I thought there could not be any difficulty. At least two other literary people had read it in typescript and their opinions were the same as the first: that it should be published. As a matter of course and of courtesy the book was sent to firms which had been producing Eleanor Farjeon's work from their Children's Departments most recently. It was returned each time with a speed so remarkable that I could only conclude it was not even being considered. It very soon began to dawn on me that there might be a rather obvious reason. These publishing houses had been selling—were still selling—Eleanor Farjeon as a CHILDREN'S WRITER and I suppose there is no "image" more important to preserve than that of the writer of children's books. So that a firm who was putting Eleanor over to a large and special public of that kind would be the last to wish at the same time to sell the story of her grown-up life.

Eleanor Farjeon was the most completely "good" person I have ever known, but she was far from "goody-goody". Children who met her loved her. But the actual story of her life and circumstances, the description of her character and ways did not altogether add up to the "image" labelled CHILDREN'S WRITER. No wonder my book was so unwelcome!

Throughout this period many people suggested to me that Sir Victor Gollancz might well look kindly on the book and I had thought so too. He had published the original edition of Eleanor's *A Nursery In The Nineties;* and she had always had a great admiration and affection for him. They both felt the same way on many matters: on loving, for instance, as opposed to hating, and on the abolition of Capital Punishment. She revered him for his championing of the defenceless peoples of the world and sympathised with his Causes generally.

There was another point, too, in favour of submitting the Memoir to Gollancz. It was a very Catholic book and I was aware from the beginning that an anti-Catholic bias could militate against its accept-ance. Anyone who has read Sir Victor Gollancz's own autobiography* or who possesses his anthologies will know that he was a liberal-minded man, sympathetic towards religion of any kind.

So *Eleanor: Portrait of a Farjeon* was sent to Sir Victor Gollancz; and on New Year's Day, 1966, I had a letter telling me that he was going to publish it.

The book came out on 7th July. By the middle of August a good crop of sympathetic reviews had appeared from various parts of the country; Neville Braybrooke had given a most sensitive talk about it on the radio; and the National Library for the Blind were planning to transcribe it into braille. This last would have pleased Eleanor Farjeon more than anything, as it did me. It made me feel once and for all that I had been justified in writing such a very personal book.

* *My Dear Timothy* and *More For Timothy.*

CHAPTER XXXII

THE FUTURE WAS beginning to look a little inactive now for one who had always craved excitement and had generally found it. But there was still a little something waiting . . .

This time it was as surprising as the poetry phase had been; although the new rôle I was about to play could not have been mine, had I not already become familiar with rhythms and the composition of verse. This fresh activity was of all things to do with music. I was to become a COMPOSER!

I must hurriedly add a composer of sorts; song-writer is really the term. But the adventures this led me into, the new people I met, the knowledge I acquired of a section of the community completely foreign to me—all this was no less exciting than my excursion into the Book Trade.

I had always had a musical ear, but no natural taste for good music. I had made ineffectual attempts to educate myself in that direction, but it was of little avail. It was not until I became friends with Eleanor Farjeon that my taste considerably improved. I have now a presentable selection of classical records; but even so they are "easy" works of a romantic nature, in which the melody is plainly discernible. With a few exceptions it is the same with poetry; I must have emotional content and a rhyming scheme.

Well, one day—I think it was the Boxing Day of 1958—I found a melody of my own. It came to me out of a title, which provided me with a good first line and the tune developed from that. Since then I have read that that most gifted of song-writers, Cole Porter, used to work in exactly this way.

It went to my head as the writing and publishing had done. I became obsessed with it and worried away at that tune on the classroom piano in the empty R.A.D.A. until at last I had produced my first song: verse, chorus and lyric all complete, all mine.

The ballad lay for several years, idle and unsold; and then a miracle happened. Cecilia appeared: a new pupil, wishing to return to the legitimate stage after a long interval. Cecilia had once been well known in the Light Entertainment world. To preserve her anonymity I call her Cecilia, after the patron saint of music. She and I became friends and partners because—and this is the miraculous part—Cecilia had also worked in the song-arranging departments of several big music publishers. There was nothing she did not know about music good and bad; and she knew exactly the shape and form that a song and its lyric must take if it is to be listened to by the popular music world. She was not without her criticisms of my ballad. Indeed, I was to learn in the forthcoming months just how much time and hard work go into the making of a popular song. It has a definite shape musically and the lyric must march with the tune and develop and come to a conclusion with it.

The song was written at last. From then onwards the usual excitements, the old familiar urgency. The first objective was to get the song professionally recorded on what is called a "demo", short for demonstration disc. I engaged two singers; I hired a studio; the demo disc was done.

Actually two songs were recorded on that day; because by then I had bought a minipiano and had written a second number, quite different from the ballad. It was very sophisticated and I was rather proud of the lyric.

The hard work was over. Now came the old question, as in the publishing world, of distribution. How was I to sell it, in fact? I made shameless use of all the people whom over many professional years I had met, and who had any connection with the world I was out to storm. But the verdict of everyone in that world coincided. The songs were not "commercial". That is to say they were unsuitable for recording for the teenager market where the money lies.

I was not surprised at this. But it had been another adventure into an unknown territory and the experience had been well worth while.

I should like to be able to point to some positive success at the end of it all, as in the other enterprises I have written about. However, I can say that at this moment one of the big recording companies, who refused the songs, have come back at me after nearly a year with a request to return both of them for reconsideration. I understand that the trend is changing and is likely to revert to the more melodious, ballad type of song in the very near future.

The effect of this has been to make me write another ballad, which I feel may be the best and certainly the most up-to-date of the three. So who knows but that by the time this book appears on the libraries' shelves, my songs, too, may be on sale in the record racks of the music shops?

*   *   *

Before I was even thirty I used to complain that life was finished, that there was nothing more to come; in those fallow periods that are part of all our lives, when nothing much seems to be happening or to be likely to happen.

A wise friend of those days used to say to me: "One door shuts; another opens." She was always proved to be right, in my case at any rate, as I think this book has shown. But now, apart from teaching and a certain continuing interest in the songs, there did not appear to be much to which I could reasonably look forward. In the summer of 1965 Eleanor Farjeon had died and as time went on I was missing her friendship more rather than less. But a door was to open twice within the coming months. The first time it led me again, strangely enough, for a brief interlude back into the sort of world which I had just been exploring. But this time it was in the way of friendship only.

The first friend I made that autumn came from America: Hildegarde, the singer. It was Eve Lavallière who brought us into each other's orbits. Hildegarde was just a name to me. I knew so little of her that when, in 1963, I saw that she was going to play Eve in a play about the famous French actress in whom I had always been so interested, I wrote to Eric Johns, editor of the *Stage* newspaper, asking him exactly who she was. He told me she was an international cabaret artist who had appeared in England more than once before the war.

About a year later I saw that Hildegarde was going to give a season at the New Arts Theatre Club. I gave her time to open and settle down and then I wrote her a letter, telling her that I knew a great deal about Lavallière and possessed the only good Life of her in English, now out of print. I told her, too, that I had some actual photographs, given me by the old French Curé who converted her, and certain relics of her actual writing and a book or two, which had come to me through the generosity of the late Bishop Craven. If she would be interested to see these things I should be delighted to show them to her.

After a little while Hildegarde wrote to me saying she would indeed be interested, although for the moment the play I spoke of had been held up. She invited me to call on her at the Arts or at the London Hippodrome where she was appearing in *Talk of the Town* the following week. I chose to go that very night to the New Arts Theatre Club.

I was fascinated with Hildegarde; I could have happily sat through her show twice over. Her pretty looks, her warmth and charm, her clear diction and beautiful singing without any question of a microphone; the whole expert professionalism of the entertainment went to make up an evening of enchantment for me.

I found her afterwards, dressing in the room I had when I played *The Magistrate;* already the fans were milling round. "Wait a bit," she said to me quietly; and when they had gone we had a short talk and arranged to meet away from the theatre later on.

After she finished at the London Hippodrome and was free in the evenings she came to the flat twice to supper and we took a great liking to her. I went more than once to see her where she was staying, off Portman Square. I was pleasantly obsessed with her. Those visits made me feel young again; like a stage-struck schoolboy, intrigued by her blonde appeal and the mystery with which that kind of celebrated Variety artist surrounds herself.

But Hildegarde and I had a great deal in common on account of our mutual Faith. She is a very devout Catholic; and underneath the thin film of Waldorf-Astoria sophistication there is still the Catholic girl from Milwaukee.

She gave me her "Album", the quaint new name for a long-playing record of selected songs. I played it a great deal while she was still here in London; but I have not yet put it on since she left. It brings her too vividly to life. . . . Perhaps I will play it again one day . . .

The other friend I made was very different from Hildegarde and belonged to the literary world, one to which by now I was quite accustomed. Her last book, *The Hound and the Falcon,* had just been published with great success and I was told I must not fail to read it. A year later she was in the news as one of the distinguished recipients of an Arts Council award. But at that time Antonia White was no more than someone well known to me as a novelist. I had never read any of her books. In fact I had always rather hurried over *White, Antonia* in the Library filing drawers; partly on account of a disinclination to read novels, and also because for so many years I had been a strict, Calvinistically-minded Roman Catholic and I had had the impression that Miss White was rather a rebel one and might be disturbing.

However, by the time *The Hound and the Falcon* came my way I had been already disturbed so much by the many changes within the Church and by my own emotional upheavals outside it that I had developed a far more liberal-minded outlook. In fact, I felt this might be just the right book at just the right moment for me. So I invested my thirty shillings. They were well spent. They were the best spent thirty shillings of my financial history. The book was splendid and honest and was all that the reviewers had said it was.

I am a slow reader of works of that kind and I took some time to finish it. But as I went on through the pages I realised that I knew the identity of the "Peter" to whom the letters were written. I also guessed that Antonia White and I would have much in common. She had suffered from nervous trouble; so had I. She had been extensively psychoanalysed; so had I. She belonged to the same Faith as I did—and had doubts; so had I.

Added to all this I gathered from the chronological table in her book that we were about the same age and had been students together at the R.A.D.A.

I sat down to write her a letter and this is what I wrote:

27 January 1966

Dear Miss White,

It seems like an act of cruelty to add to the stream of fan-mail which I'm sure your last book has produced; but I feel I must tell you how *much* I've enjoyed those letters.

They've been in some way a comfort and a great help. For they treat of so many things which I understand, sympathise with and suffer from myself—as a convert from 1934, and as a psychiatric subject since 1904!

There is, too, always a kind of egotistical pleasure in reading of someone who is about one's own age, and who has travelled rather the same sort of path and has probably known many of the same people as oneself. I was in and out of the B.B.C. in the Drama and Features departments during the War when you were there; and you began at the R.A.D.A. in the year that I left—at the end of the Summer Term. You must have been there with Flora Robson?

I imagine the anonymity of "Peter" is for the greater reading public. I think he must be someone whom, as an actor, I always knew of and whom Eleanor Farjeon used to tell me a lot about. She was my greatest woman friend for the last fifteen years of her life which ended in the summer. She became a Catholic in the first two years of our friendship and was a particularly wonderful person to whom I owe more than I can ever say. As I read your letters I kept thinking how Eleanor would have loved them. She read a great deal. Her own letters were remarkable and I've been able to make use of them in a Memoir which Gollancz is doing in July. Eleanor suffered from many physical disabilities latterly, but did not know what "nerves" were; however, she suffered them and bore them in and for me with heroic patience and unselfishness.

I've already prayed for you more than once and hope things are a little more peaceful now. I've found the spirit of Joy is the "Fruit" to try to cultivate—joy as opposed to happiness, a very different thing.

Many good wishes and many thanks,

Yours sincerely,

Denys Blakelock

This was her reply, which to my delight came winging by return:

30 January 1966

Dear Denys Blakelock,

It is true that I *have* had a great many letters about my book but none could have come as a more delightful surprise than yours. You see I am a very old admirer of yours and for many years now have delighted in your splendid performances on radio. I remember you very well indeed at the R.A.D.A. as the most brilliant young man in the "Finals"; and you are one of the few who were there in my time who really made their mark in the theatre. Yes, I was there with Flora Robson, the shining light in our group, and with Colin Clive whom I did meet again years afterwards.

I cannot tell you how much your letter moved me and interested me. I had no idea that you were a Catholic, still less that you were a "psychiatric subject". You have *all* my sympathy about the latter— it really is an affliction, isn't it? I've recently become involved in all that old trouble again, just when I fondly hoped I was tolerably free of it.

How interesting that Eleanor Farjeon was such a great friend of yours. I never met her but I had a great admiration for her and always felt she must be a wonderful person. I had no idea that she had become a Catholic. I look forward very much to your Memoir of her. I am always deeply impressed by people who suffer physical disabilities heroically, being an abject physical coward myself. I've been lucky about physical illness, though not quite so lucky about the other kind.

A letter like yours is a great help and comfort to *me*. It makes me feel less odd and less isolated. Thank you *very* much for your prayers. I rather need them at this moment. I feel in my bones that you are right about the spirit of Joy being the Fruit to try to cultivate—joy as opposed to "happiness". God must have inspired you to say just that to me at this particular moment when I am inwardly oppressed and *de*pressed.

Thank you *very* much for writing to me. Your letter was such a lovely surprise and "made my day" yesterday. I wonder if we shall ever meet again. It would give me great pleasure, having already had so much pleasure from your work. But now you are a real person for me, not just a brilliant actor and I have gained immensely.

Yours very gratefully,

Antonia White

We continued to correspond and at first I was inclined to let my old enemy, urgency, press home too hard and too quickly. I would answer poor Antonia White's letters before the sun had gone down behind the nearest pillar box. But I soon saw the red light and pulled up. I reduced my letters in length and in frequency.

The evening arrived when she first came to supper. I had cooked my best-occasion casserole the previous day and was ready long before the time in a state of high expectancy. As she came through the front door I recognised her at once. "Why, we know each other!" I said. I remembered her distinctly over forty years, as a very pretty, very fair girl called "Tony", but then she had a different surname.

After that our friendship—galloped ahead? I would rather say "cantered", because it travelled swiftly but without excitement. It was steady, even, undemanding on either side. In one of her earliest letters Antonia was already agreeing with me that "something quietly lasting has been brought into being". We had both led *un*quiet lives of interior conflict, had had many relationships that were clamorous and involved. So both of us now felt grateful for a friendship that was non-emotional, serene and unsentimental.

CHAPTER XXXIII

IT SEEMS TO have been my good fortune to have found as friends especially gifted people at the start of their careers. I have written about Laurence Olivier as I knew him in his young days. Now I should like to say something about two other great friends: one already established, whom I have known for nearly twenty years, the other who is fast making his name, who has been a friend of mine for no more than seven or eight.

The first is James Roose-Evans, Director of the Hampstead Theatre Club and prime mover of its inception. I met Jimmie in 1948, when he was just past his twenty-first birthday. At that time he had not even decided to adopt the theatre as his career. But after going up to Oxford and taking his degree he made the choice that was for him inevitable. If ever a man was made and meant for the theatre it was Jimmie Roose-Evans.

Before many years had gone by he began to drift in the direction of production, his first important post of that kind being at the Maddermarket Theatre, Norwich. There he gained invaluable experience of directing a company; and because it is made up of anonymous amateurs Jimmie has always been sympathetic towards the amateur movement.

He has taught a great deal: in America and here, at the R.A.D.A. and the Central. He is a practical idealist and has a special appeal for students and young actors, who find in his unwearying pursuit of his own particular Grail a source of inspiration and a spur to industry.

One could not but admire Jimmie, because he has consistently and over a great number of years put his highly creative gifts at the disposal of the theatre, without consideration of financial gain or personal glorification. He is a great worker and started the Hampstead Theatre Club on a very short shoestring indeed. It was a long struggle and he did not spare himself. Now, at last, he has begun to reap the reward. Many plays have been transferred from Hampstead to the West End; and recently his all-star production of *The Ideal Husband* has put him firmly in his rightful place among the top theatre directors.

Jimmie is at his best when his imagination is stretched to its limits, as in the case of *The Little Clay Cart*, an ancient Indian play that he unearthed and adapted for the British theatre. Although, as usual, he had to do it on a minimum budget, the magic and the beauty he somehow managed to conjure up on that tiny stage could not have been equalled by a Peter Brook, with Drury Lane and all the money and talents in the world at his command. It would be ungrateful, however, in the case of *The Little Clay Cart*, to make no mention of Barbara Wilkes's décor, which was as exquisite as it was resourceful.

Jimmie Roose-Evans is catholic in his theatre tastes and has had equal success with the revival of Coward's *Private Lives* and pieces of the poetic school such as *Cider With Rosie* and *Under Milk Wood*. He would say that when first we met he had a good deal to learn from me about the theatre's ways and means. Now I could teach him nothing. On the contrary, I would say that James Roose-Evans has a wider and deeper experimental knowledge of the theatre and all its allied arts than anyone in this country today.

The other friend with special talents whose beginnings I have seen is David Pinner.

It is customary, in writing books of this kind, to include only those whose names will be of exceptional interest to most readers: those, in fact, who have "arrived". I would like to depart from this custom and take a chance on the future news value of a young author who cannot yet be said to have quite "arrived", but who gives every appearance of being about to do so. To "arrive" in any medium it needs that one particular play, that single special performance that suddenly brings the author or the actor right up to the very front. From then on he becomes a "name" with the public and a proposition to managers and agents. He is no longer seeking, he is sought after. Christopher Fry with *The Lady's Not For Burning* could have been said to have "arrived". David Pinner has not quite made that peak point yet. But he is prolific and young and may well have done so before this book can reach the Libraries.

David was in my class at the R.A.D.A. in 1959. He is a very good actor and at any time might prove himself to be a top-ranking one. But it is in relation to his gifts as a writer and poet that he shows all the signs of excelling. He is now only twenty-five and has already written ten plays and approximately two hundred poems. In 1965 he was given a bursary of £500 by the Arts Council, in order to make it possible for him to continue with his writing. Up to June 1966, he has had a play, *Dickon*, produced at the Queen's Theatre, Hornchurch and on the B.B.C.'s Third Programme. It has also been accepted for publication, together with two others, *Fanghorn* and *The Drums of Snow*, by Penguin Books. His novel, *Ritual*, is to be published by Hutchinson in October 1967.

David Pinner pushed his way into my life in a manner quite unusual in a student. I did not make it my habit to invite my R.A.D.A. pupils to the flat. With David I did not have to invite him; he asked himself. First he brought his poetry; then he brought his girls. Then he started writing plays and brought all three.

David has that way which I have observed in young people who are teeming with creative energy: they never stop to think about being refused or rebuffed. They ask, they take. In varying degrees I used to notice this with Laurence Olivier and with James Roose-Evans in their youth. Like David, they were blunt—inconsiderate in its literal meaning. They did not stop to consider. David Pinner tempers this quality with an extraordinary kindness and warmth. Like the others he is prodigal with his affections. They are generous, these strange beings. They would be, of course. Meanness comes from caution; they are incautious.

David used to come to supper and read his poems to me. His fecundity as a poet has always been immense. I must say that he listened too, and attentively, to mine. His intellect, his taste, and his whole poetic vision are far beyond my reach. But he is not a culture snob and was able to find many things to like in my verses. The poetry readings were intense; David reading his to me in his *vox humana*, I mine to him in my *vox celeste*.

There was a near-disastrous evening when David read me a very long poem indeed. It took about twenty minutes to speak. The room was hot; the wine had flowed; the day had been long and exhausting. I heard the first few lines, then knew no more till I came up from a deep sleep as the poet spoke his final precious words.

"Denys! You were asleep."

"David—oh, David, please, please forgive me . . . Show me that you do by reading it again."

He did. He read it again . . . and I went to sleep again.

David married, in 1965, Catherine, by whom he must have been inspired to write many poems. She is a great beauty, and so much more than that, with her intelligence, her gentleness and humour. She is also gifted in the field of music. This is not surprising as she is the daughter of that great artist, Sidney Griller, who has delighted music lovers all the world over with his concerts. Even a musical Philistine like myself has always known the name of the Griller String Quartet.

Sidney is a most endearing character. A virtuoso on the platform, he proved a perilous fellow motorist on the Mile End Road. We hired a car between us to go to Hornchurch to see David's play, *Dickon*. I was at the wheel and Sidney, sitting in the back, acted as Guide to the City and to East London where he was born. We took half an hour, touring wildly round the maze of one-way streets, before we could get even to Aldgate; with Sidney Griller reminiscing and pointing out the old familiar landmarks as we went.

CHAPTER XXXIV

Several years have been skipped over and purposely; chronological order being less important than to cover all I have had to say about each particular ploy in which I have been engaged and finish with it.

So here shall come an extraordinary interlude: an account of strange happenings which, when I look back on them, I can hardly believe ever took place. In strict order of time they properly belong to a period several years earlier: to 1959.

In October 1959 I fell in love. I fell in love with a house. It was in Hampstead. In common with many other people I had always wanted one—of the cottage variety—up in that district and now I found it; although it could hardly be described as a cottage. It was, in fact, a studio, designed for a rich painter called Gluck in her garden in the Windmill Hill area just below the Heath. It came to my notice in the usual manner: through an advertisement in a Sunday newspaper.

It must be plain by now that I am not one to waste time. I viewed it the next morning at midday, bathed in the brilliant October sunshine. I was to learn later that that was the one short space in the day when the sun shone in such a way as to light up the corners of that high, cavernous building. But as I saw it then it is not too much to say that I fell in love with it.

It can be dangerous to fall in love with a human being; more dangerous to fall in love with a house; and more dangerous still to buy it in twenty minutes. But that is what I did.

For the three weeks following it was like a love affair—an infatuation. Friends and relatives warned me from every direction. "You won't be lonely, will you? It will be a very different life," they said, "for a bachelor who has lived for twenty years in a centrally heated block of flats in the middle of London." I was reminded, too, of the porters we had, to take in parcels and messages; and the two shops in the entrance hall, which made housekeeping so easy.

But I would have none of it. I was besotted. Urgency was becoming more and more urgent. I hustled my solicitors along; and when they talked in cautious legal tones and mentioned something called "searches", I cried, "What do you want to *search* for? I've done all that!" I had indeed been to the Town Hall and found out the history of the studio, built in the 1930's, and had been assured that there were no building plans whatsoever that could spoil this little country corner. The sale was nearly through, in fact, when one evening I went up to see the "Vendor" (as the owner was called); and as the "Purchaser" (that was me) sat there in the dusk his spirits sank perceptibly. It seemed so dim. Even when the crude centre light and a little concealed lighting were turned on, it struck me now as dismal and removed. It was hard to recognise the studio I had seen so short a time before, cheerful, welcoming and filled with warm sunshine.

When I left the studio that evening it was dark. My mind was dark, too, with thoughts of what life might be going to be after all, up there alone on Windmill Hill.

However, I felt I had gone too far. In another week the sale was through; and on the morning I went up to Hampstead, a man of property for the first time in my life, my heart was heavier than lead. I turned the key in the door, and oh! what desolation was there before me: the desolation of a completely empty house, the stained, disfigured walls stripped of the pictures and bookshelves and curtains; of all that had gone to make it a home, friendly and lived-in.

I stood looking up through the ugly North window and saw before me an eight foot wall. It was prison! Why hadn't I noticed it before? In a few moments a woman friend, Sally Thomas, joined me and I fancied that her tones of enthusiasm were a little forced. "It's lovely," she cried. "But is it?" I replied with an insistent query. I drew her to the window and pointing at the wall said, "Wormwood Scrubs, don't you think?"

We looked about: up into the musicians' gallery, made much of in the advertisement and where my predecessor had slept (there was no real bedroom); into the kitchen and bathroom that were on either side of the glass doors leading into the garden; and finally out into the garden itself. The weather was dark and the lily pond—also a great feature—had lost its fascination for me. I took my friend back into the house; and standing once more beneath the wall in the gloomy North light I said, "I'm not going to live here, you know."

Five minutes later I was on the telephone, instructing the Insurance Company to change the coverage from permanent to temporary. The studio was up for sale.

Before long a purchaser was found, and while he was looking for a mortgage I was desperately seeking for another flat in central London. It seemed a hopeless task. So apparently proved the mortgage; for a few days before Christmas, the purchaser telephoned to tell me he could not raise the sum and that I must consider myself free to sell elsewhere.

A friend of mine was there when I put down the receiver. "You don't sound very disappointed," he said. "I'm not," I replied, "I'm going to live there myself after all."

To those who might accuse me of infirmity of purpose I can only reply: not at all. My fruitless experience of flat-hunting had driven me back on to this home that was mine and empty and holding out its arms to me. I decided to spend more money (I little thought how much) and convert the dark, gaunt studio into a light, elegant and homely house.

The day before Christmas Eve I met the builder and we discussed plans. "Put a floor in," I said airily; for that would give me a picture-window looking upwards towards the Heath. "Raise the roof," he warned me, "to comply with the by-laws." I little thought what *that* meant; but the spending-lust was on, and from that time forth money was no object. Fitted carpets of broadloom and antique furniture of every kind were ordered without regard to cost. I collected enough chairs to hold a committee meeting; and luxurious lamps were bought to shed their radiance from every shelf and table. I left out nothing; anxiety alone provided for every possible contingency. I even ordered (a mere £125) a balustrade, and a delicate white wrought-iron stair-case to lead from the epistyle outside my bedroom window down to the garden beneath. This was supposed to be ready and in place by September, 1960.

I myself moved in on 26th July, although the house was not nearly ready for me. 26th July. Moving day! Trying not to fuss the men, I anxiously watched my antique pieces being carried out like corpses. I saw my beautiful china being perilously wrapped in tattered pages of the *News of the World* and the *Daily Mirror* and bundled into a crate. I saw my irreplaceable clothes laid flat upon the floor and folded into some grubby old piece of material. Where, oh where, were the ward-robe-suitcases I had been told of? ("Leave it all to the removal men", they had said. "They'll do everything.") The carpets were taken up, none too carefully (one was torn up at a corner) and the evacuation was complete. The flat I had lived in for twenty years and where so much had happened to me was empty, and I was nothing but glad to turn my back on it and go. It was farewell for ever to Endsleigh Court.

The actual moving-in to Windmill Hill was rather gay. It did not take long, and when it was over I had bottles of beer waiting for the men. We had quite a party. In fact, the removal men seemed to enjoy themselves so much that I began to fear I should never get the removers to remove. They had finished their job for the day; but all the work-men were still hard at it and I was anxious to give them their celebration-party too.

"Well," I said, "I suppose I ought to be getting on." They took the hint and soon there was the sound of the van moving off down the hill.

Then the real party began. All tools were laid down and Tom, Dick, Bert and Harry raised their glasses, brimming over with cider and ales light and brown. I had invited anyone who had played any part at all in the conversion of the house, and one by one they arrived from their various building-sites and jobs in the surrounding district.

During the general conversation the subject of wives and marriages inevitably came up. Having by now had a good many drinks, I confessed to having been engaged to be married but once in my life, and that only for forty-eight hours. Eyebrows went up all round; and I knew the men were curious to know the why and the wherefore. "You see," I explained, "the lady alarmed me. When I asked her if she would be my wife she cried, Yes! Then, flinging her arms round my neck, she cried, *Now I'll never let you go!*" This confession from my past brought forth a "belly laugh" from the all-male assembly.

The party was a great success and I felt it was a wonderful start off to my new life.

For the next many weeks I lived on the first floor only, without carpets or curtains. Here I planned and picnicked and gave speech lessons, while the workmen continued to finish the ground floor rooms and to paint the outside of the house. This, though exhausting, was a novel and exciting period, and I looked forward to letting the work-men in at eight o'clock every morning; it gave the house a feeling of life and friendliness. Often in the middle of the day I would have lunch at a pub with the builder and his wife and daughter, and discuss further plans for spending more money, though he would try to restrain me. "That's my last extravagance," I would say; and I said it many times.

But at last the house was finished, except for the outside staircase, the workmen were gone and I was left alone. It certainly looked lovely; especially the first-floor room in front. But once having created it, it always seemed to me more like a theatre-set than a home; and although I should have enjoyed acting in that room I never really wanted to live in it.

However, for the moment I was too busy preparing for the Hampstead house-warming of a hundred people to think about the place in terms of life; and there were friends coming and going all the time to help me and keep me company. The day came at last and the catering firm did their job magnificently. The rooms and staircases were filled with brightly-coloured chrysanthemums; and outside, to the wall (which I had now come to like) white wooden trellises had been fastened, from which Victorian baskets of yellow button-chrysanthemums, bedded in moss, cascaded trailing ivy. The wines, red and white, flowed freely. The party was a success. The last guests went, and I was really alone at last.

One of my friends had said as he was going, "It's funny, isn't it—a house-warming? You build a beautiful home and then immediately invite your friends to ruin it for you."

At the time I thought this a rather dampening thing to say, but when I had closed the door on the last guest and was left alone in the house, I began to see the truth of his remark. The place was littered with ashes and cigarette stubs, burned-out matches and discarded orange-sticks, smears of lipstick on the white paint, and deep crimson wine-stains on the carpet. It was a revelation to me. But it had to be dealt with at once; and I was brushing and scraping, scrubbing and sponging, till 1.0 a.m. in the morning. Then and then only did I feel I could climb into bed; and I soon sank into a contented sleep.

As I went drowsily off I thought of the evening's events, and I felt that it had been a good beginning to a new phase. The future looked hopeful and rosy. I had found the right home in the right place and the way of life that suited me at last.

CHAPTER XXXV

BY RIGHTS I should have slept long and wakened the next morning and lived through that day in a cocoon of continuing contentment. Nothing of the kind. I awoke early in an acute state of anxiety, and with the symptoms of guilty conscience already aflame. How *could* I have spent so much money? Especially on that display of flowers, when there were people starving and destitute, or living at best in great poverty in every corner of the world? Those Victorian baskets alone . . .

Then I was assailed by misgivings of a more selfish nature. I had spent so prodigally from the start, how was I going to live up here amongst a lot of well-to-do people? How was I going to keep up with the Joneses of Hampstead? And did I believe that that was the right way to live anyhow?

There was one part-solution. I could let the ground-floor flatlet at once. This had been referred to during the building period first as Roger the Lodger's room, and finally as just "Roger's" room.

So now I cried aloud, "I must find Roger the Lodger at once," and leaped from the bed and into my clothes. "*He* will help me to pay my way."

Into the car and up to London and on to a well-known accommodation bureau. There was a pathetically long queue of would-be tenants waiting patiently for addresses, but no one who looked like a suitable lodger for me. Not a Roger to be seen.

"Would you take a lady?" said the girl at the desk.

"A lady . . . oh . . . er, would she want a bath?"

"Well, it is usual."

"Oh . . . is it?"

"Well, I've always had one," the young lady replied coldly.

"But you see, the trouble is that there is only a shower in the flatlet. The bathroom leads off my own bedroom. So you see . . . it wouldn't be quite *comme il faut*, do you think? One lady friend of mine did suggest something she called "making an arrangement" that alarmed me exceedingly. What could I arrange? You see, I use my bedroom so much as a work-room that a regular rota would be hard to set down. When the lady wanted her bath . . . I . . . well I might be out . . . or I might be in . . ."

"Mr. Blakelock!"

"Oh, not in the bath," I said hurriedly. (I was getting thoroughly flustered.) "I mean I might be having to write in my room, or to change or wanting a bath myself. . . . You do see, don't you?

The young woman at the desk, plainly a feminist, gazed at me glassily, implacably.

"Very well," I said, going down like an Aunt Sally. "Put them both on the list, men and women, and see what results we get."

With this I clumsily backed from the gaze of this basilisk, and in a dark mood of foreboding drove myself home up to Hampstead.

Two days passed with the telephone constantly ringing. But when they knew there was only a shower and no bath, or the use of one, everybody shied off—especially the women. On the third day, however, a man called, an army officer, who seemed rather to like the flatlet, but he telephoned later to say that he had made other plans and that the room was a little too small for his taste.

The great rains that had begun on the morning of the party had settled into a ceaseless downpour. It was practically tropical, and it may be remembered that it went on and on and on by day and by night, until in the end one could not believe it would ever stop. It was an unfortunate beginning for me. I don't like rain.

Then again, while I was waiting to hear from the officer, I began for the first time to envisage what a lodger in the house might mean. The walls were far from sound-proof. He could be a wireless fiend or a television addict. Or worse? I was completely cut off in that corner. Perhaps I should be bashed or coshed, or have a flick-knife applied to my windpipe?

When the officer refused I was relieved beyond measure. I decided to temporise and think no more about a lodger till I had got myself settled down.

Once, during the unhappy weeks after the party, I had reason to telephone to the head porter of Endsleigh Court. He said, "Gladdy would like to have a word with you." Gladdy was one of the cleaners who had been there longest and who had worked for me for some time. She now said down the telephone, " 'Ow are yer, dearie?"

"Oh, all right, Gladdy," I replied.

"Dontcher miss us, dear?" she asked me.

"Yes, I do rather, Gladdy," I said, keeping a stiff upper lip.

"I thoughtcher would, dear," and she was gone.

Gladdy's worldly wisdom had taught her that one becomes painfully attached to the people around you and to the customs and scenes of a particular neighbourhood.

These were bad days. On the third night after the party my spirits, that had continued so high and (for me) so long, began to sink, down and down and down to zero point. Without relief I was enveloped by a dark cloud of deep depression. I missed the guests, I missed the workmen. The silence and the aloneness gave me a sense of what it must be like to be a lighthouse-keeper. I even missed the noise.

From that time onward the cloud never lifted, until one day, only four weeks after the house-warming, I had to face the fact that I had made the biggest and most expensive mistake of my life. I felt lonely, cut off, and very cold, after twenty years of life in a warm flat, surrounded by people, with my brother and his wife always at hand. The day came when I sat eating my solitary lunch, looking out at what had been a beautiful country scene, now shrouded by sheets of blinding rain, and found myself saying out loud, "I hate it here! I *hate* it here!" I hurriedly finished my meal and went to the telephone. I asked the Estate Agent to come up at once and discuss a matter of great urgency. Half an hour later the house was up for sale.

When a few days afterwards I ran into the local reporter I said, "I'm getting out of this place. It's like living on the slopes of Snowdonia." He staggered slightly, as it was only a month since he had reported my successful arrival at Hampstead in his column, "Heathman's Diary".

He came up to tea to hear more. As luck would have it while he was there Yehudi Menuhin's daughter, soon to be married to Fou Ts'ong, called to see the studio with a view to making it their home. She was charming. I fell in love with her and she fell in love with the house, as I had done. She begged me not to let it go until her father and her fiancé had been to see it. This exciting occasion, however, never came to pass. She telephoned to say that from her description they had decided that the house was too small for their purpose; that a pianist must have a music room where he can practise undisturbed.

This colourful and unexpected visit was a windfall for the Hampstead reporter. Not only did an account appear in the column of his own local paper, but the following morning there was a paragraph in "Tanfield's Diary" in the *Daily Mail*. This proved to be an embarrassment to the Menuhin family and to me too, as the enormous price I started at, and didn't get, spread about the impression that I was very wealthy. Sir Robert Shone, who bought the house eventually and is a good businessman, reduced the sum considerably. My friend the builder had warned me all along that I was spending so wildly that I would be unlikely to get my money back, much less make a profit.

However, I just about broke even and considered myself lucky to do that. It had been a salutary experience.

One pouring wet day before I left Hampstead I was paying a roundsman his bill at the door. I told him I was already leaving. "What?" he cried. "You must be crazy." Then he added with the most twinkling of winks, "What *you* want is a couple o' nice 'ousekeepers." The housekeeper idea was a good one, if I could have afforded to pay her. But why did I need two, I wondered? It sounded a little Turkish to me.

I asked him if he himself would like to live up in this country district. "Not me," he cried, "give me the good old Kilburn 'Igh Road, with people about, and the 'buses and shops, and a picture palace just round the corner."

"There you are, you see," I said, "I'm not so crazy after all."

When the news of my imminent departure appeared in the *Ham and High* (Hampstead and Highgate Express) it caused a minor sensation. One wit suggested I should now give a farewell party.

Meanwhile I was descending with my usual urgency on various districts of central London. In the end and quite soon I learned of a flat that was likely to be vacant in a week or two. It was in the very block I had left only six months before. I pounced and I paid and I planned. Before many days had passed, carpenters, painters, plumbers and the layers of oilcloth were once more at work for me. I repeated the pattern of the studio, and had magnolia-white walls in the one room and hall, primrose yellow in bathroom and kitchen.

It was right on the front, on the main road, a quite new departure for me. But I had double windows installed and I came to the conclusion then that I preferred the noise of London traffic to the disturbance of neighbours playing their mechanical toys; record players, television, radios, through the adjoining wall. My bathroom insulated me on one side; my neighbour's bathroom on the other. This meant I had no living-room noises next to mine whatever.

I was back where I belonged; I hoped I might never have to move away from there again.

My return journey from Hampstead to Bloomsbury was less gay, but viewed from a distance more amusing.

This time I made the fatal mistake of economising. Instead of the big removal firm of renown, I was persuaded to engage a little man round the corner, who was nevertheless reputed to be used to removals of good furniture; and I was assured had a van so large that he had recently been able to move the contents of a five-roomed flat.

John Neville in *Alfie*, 1963

Peter O'Toole in the film, *Great Catherine*, 1967

He turned up punctually with a van about the size of that used by the Scarlet Pimpernel to convey his refugees out of Paris. Into this, with the help of his mate, who proved to be only a café acquaintance willing to oblige, he stuffed my precious belongings, till by one o'clock he had reached saturation point. There were still some of my best pieces standing sorrowfully out in the open on Windmill Hill. It was impossible to be angry with the two men; they were so determinedly amiable and touching. They were like two characters from *Waiting for Godot*.

They somehow managed to squeeze in the remainder, at great cost to the polished furniture and newly-painted bookshelves, and off they trundled to Bloomsbury. Once there—it was now 1.30 p.m.—I plied them with ham sandwiches and whisky. Having done justice to this informal meal, the smaller of the two, the assistant, announced that he had to go, as he was helping an exponent of Yoga as an afternoon job. This was unanswerable and I had to be content to arrange with them to return at 5.30 to move me in. When they did, unable to park in the street, they drove the heavily-loaded van into the garage beneath the block of flats.

This final operation was done to the accompaniment of cider and cake. At last I bade them a friendly, if not affectionate, farewell. I heard afterwards that their van, being relieved of the weight of my belongings, had risen in an offended fashion to the roof of the garage under the flats, where it became immovable. It couldn't be induced to budge, much to the chagrin of the head porter and to the tenants of the garage as they drove in one by one.

The situation was only saved by my poor "Godots" having to let the air out of all the four tyres, thereby lowering the van from its dignified height and releasing it from its embrace with the roof.

My own personal departure from the Studio House after the Godots had gone had about it a faint inverted echo of the closing moments of *The Cherry Orchard*. The day before I moved out two of the workmen returned; and, as at the last moment I urgently gathered together my remaining belongings, there was the sound of rhythmic knocking on the peaceful air. But it was nothing so beautiful or so symbolic as the felling of a cherry tree. It was only my delicate, white, wrought-iron outside staircase, arrived three months too late and looking like a large red fire escape, being riveted into place.

CONCLUSION

"I WAS BACK where I belonged; I hoped I might never have to move away from there again."

That was undoubtedly what I felt at the relief of finding myself, that cold February, on familiar ground; in the same building once again with my brother and his wife and in the warmth of a centrally-heated flat. But things were to turn out very differently; and in two years from that time I found myself on the move again. A change in our domestic situation brought about a family exodus from Blooms-bury. We combined forces for the first time and settled in a large flat in St. Petersburgh Place, immediately opposite the Synagogue: on the wrong side of the Park but at the right end of Bayswater. The flat has a charming aspect, the luxury of two bathrooms and is easily divisible. Alban and Renée live at one end, I at the other. We are old enough and wise enough to be able to share the large kitchen in amity. It all works splendidly.

For me it is the most tranquil period in my life. I enjoy living in a more communal manner. I was not meant to live alone. Across the road there is a garden that belongs to me and I do not even have to pay a man to keep it up—Kensington Gardens.

I have come to appreciate happiness of a serener kind at last. And in any case I think there cannot be much left now: the daily round and a few minor pleasures. The books have been written, the songs composed. Old friends have gone; and of the new the last latecomer, surely, must have arrived? The parts have all been played. The peacock cannot strut again; there is but one rôle left to the sparrow now—the owl. I wonder . . . when this my summing-up is finished, what more will there be for me to do? Will all the excitements be really over? Who knows? Even now there may be *something* waiting round the next corner. . . .